The God of All Comfort

Hannah Whitall Smith

□ *Whitaker House*

THE GOD OF ALL COMFORT

ISBN: 0-88368-496-9
Printed in the United States of America
Copyright © 1984 by Whitaker House

Whitaker House
30 Hunt Valley Circle
New Kensington, PA 15068

5 6 7 8 9 10 11 12 13 14 / 06 05 04 03 02 01 00 99 98 97

CONTENTS

Chapter 1

THE REASON FOR THIS BOOK

"My heart is inditing a good matter: I speak of the things which I have made touching the king"—Psalm 45:1.

I was once talking about Christianity with an intelligent agnostic, whom I very much wished to influence. After listening to me politely for a little while, he said, "Well, madam, all I have to say is this. If you Christians want to make us agnostics inclined to look into your religion, you must try and be more comfortable in the possession of it yourselves. The Christians I meet seem to me to be the most uncomfortable people anywhere around. They seem to carry their religion as a man carries a headache. He does not want to get rid of his head, but at the same time it is very uncomfortable to have it. And I for one do not care to have that sort of religion."

This was a lesson I have never forgotten, and it is my primary reason for writing this book.

I was a very young Christian at the time of this

conversation, and I was still experiencing the first joy of my new birth. Consequently, I could not believe that any of God's children could be as uncomfortable in their religious lives as my agnostic friend claimed. But when the early glow of my conversion faded, I came down to the dullness of everyday duties and responsibilities. I soon found that there was far too much truth in his assertion. The religious life of most of us was full of discomfort and unrest. It seemed, as one of my Christian friends said to me, "as if we had just enough religion to make us miserable."

I confess that this was very disappointing, for I expected something completely different. The Bible declares the fruit of the Christian life to be love and joy and peace. But instead of the Biblical fruit, Christians often develop doubt, fear, unrest, conflict, and discomfort of every kind.

Why should the children of God lead spiritually uncomfortable lives when He has led us to believe that His yoke would be easy and His burden light? Why are we tormented with so many doubts and heavy anxieties? Why do we find it difficult to be sure that God truly loves us? Why is it that we never seem able to believe in His kindness and His care? How can we suspect Him of forgetting us and forsaking us in times of need? We trust our earthly friends and feel comfortable with them. Why is it that we cannot trust our heavenly Friend and that we are uncomfortable in His service?

I believe I have found the answer to these questions. My purpose in writing this book is to bring genuine comfort into some troubled Christian lives. I am convinced that the spiritual life of a follower of the Lord Jesus Christ was meant to be full of comfort. Furthermore, I believe that every newly converted soul, in the first joy of its conversion, fully expects such a life. And yet, for a large proportion of Christians, their religious lives are the most uncomfortable part of their existence. Is this the Lord's fault? Has He promised more than He is able to supply?

God Keeps His Promises

A late writer said, "We know what over-advertisement is. It is a twentieth-century disease from which we all suffer. There are posters on every billboard, exaggerations on every blank wall, representations and misrepresentations without number."

Is it the same with the Kingdom of God? Do the fruits we raise from the good seed of the Kingdom agree with the description given by Him who gave us that good seed? Has He misled us?

There are some who believe that Christ has offered in His gospel more than He has to give. People admit that they have not experienced what was predicted as the portion of the children of God. But why is this so? Has the Kingdom of God been over-advertised or is it only that it has been under-believed? Has the Lord Jesus Christ been over-estimated, or has He only been under-trusted?

I firmly believe that the Kingdom of God could not possibly be over-advertised nor the Lord Jesus Christ over-estimated. "Eye hath not seen, nor ear heard, neither have entered into the heart of man, the things which God hath prepared for them that love Him" (1 Corinthians 2:9). All the difficulty arises from the fact that we have under-believed and under-trusted.

In the Lord Jesus Christ, there is a deep and lasting peace and comfort of soul which nothing earthly can disturb. It belongs to those who embrace it. If this is our rightful portion, we must learn how to receive it and what things hinder its becoming a reality in our lives. There is God's part in the matter, and there is man's part. We must look carefully at both.

A wild, young fellow was brought to the Lord at a mission meeting and became a rejoicing Christian. He lived an exemplary life afterward and was asked by someone what he did to get converted. "Oh," he said, "I did my part, and the Lord did His."

"But what was your part," asked the inquirer, "and what was the Lord's part?"

"My part," he replied promptly, "was to run away, and the Lord's part was to run after me, until He caught me." A most significant answer, but how few can understand it.

God's part is always to run after us. Christ came to seek and to save that which was lost. "What man of you," He says, "having an hundred sheep, if he lose one of them, doth not leave the ninety and nine in the wilderness, and go after that which is lost until he find it? And when he hath found it, he layeth it on his shoulders, rejoicing" (Luke 15:4).

This is always the divine part, but in our foolishness we do not understand it. We think that the Lord is the one who is lost and that our part is to seek and find Him. The very expressions we use show this. We urge sinners to "seek the Lord," and we talk about having "found" Him.

"Have you found the Savior?" asked a zealous mission worker of a happy, trusting little girl. With a look of amazement, she replied in a tone of wonder, "Why, I did not know the Savior was lost!"

Misconceptions And Confusion

It is our ignorance of God that causes the problem. Because we do not know Him, we naturally get all sorts of wrong ideas about Him. We think He is an angry Judge who is on the watch for our slightest faults or a harsh Taskmaster determined to exact from us the uttermost service. We imagine Him as a self-absorbed Deity, demanding His full measure of honor and glory or as far-off Sovereign concerned only with His own affairs and indifferent to our welfare. Who can wonder that such a God can neither be loved nor trusted? And who could expect Christians with such ideas concerning Him to be anything but full of discomfort and misery?

It is impossible for anyone who truly knows God to have any such uncomfortable thoughts about Him. Plenty of outward discomforts may exist and, with them, many earthly sorrows and trials. But through it all, the soul that knows God can dwell in a fortress of perfect peace.

"But whoso hearkeneth unto me shall dwell safely, and shall be quiet from fear of evil" (Proverbs 1:33). This is a statement that no one dare question. We must listen to God, not only hearing Him, but believing what we hear. Then we would know that because He is God, He cannot do anything other than care for us as He cares for the apple of His eye. All that tenderest love and divine wisdom can do for our welfare must be and will be done without fail. Not a single loophole for worry or fear is left to the soul that knows God.

"Ah yes," you say, "but how am I to get to know Him? Other people seem to have some kind of inward revelation that makes them know Him, but I never do. No matter how much I pray, everything seems dark to me. I want to know God, but I do not see how I can manage it."

Your trouble is that you have gotten a wrong idea of what knowing God is. I am not writing about any mystical interior revelations of any kind. Such revelations are delightful when you have them, but they are often variable and uncertain. The kind of knowing I mean is just the plain, matter-of-fact knowledge of God's nature and character. It comes to us by believing what is revealed to us in the Bible concerning Him.

The apostle John says at the close of his gospel, "And many other signs truly did Jesus in the presence of his disciples, which are not written in this book: But these are written that ye might believe that Jesus is the Christ, the Son of God; and that believing ye might have life through his name" (John 20:30-31). It is believing what is written, not what is inwardly revealed, that gives life. The kind of knowing I mean comes from believing the things that are written.

The Reliable Bible

When I read in the Bible that God is love, I am to believe it because it is written, and not because I have any inward revelation that it is true. When the Bible says that He cares for us as He cares for the lilies of the field and the birds of the air and that the very hairs of our heads are all numbered, I am to believe it, just because it is written. It does not matter whether I have any inward revelation of it or not.

It is of vital importance for us to understand that the Bible is a statement, not of theories, but of actual facts. Things are not true because they are in the Bible, but they are only in the Bible because they are true.

A little boy, who had been studying at school about the discovery of America, said to his father one day, "Father, if I had been Columbus, I would not have taken all that trouble to discover America."

"Why, what would you have done?" asked the father.

"Oh," replied the little boy, "I would just have gone to the map and found it."

This little boy did not understand that maps are only pictures of already known places. America did not exist because it was on the map; but it could not be on the map until it was already known to exist.

The Bible, like the map, is a simple statement of facts. When it tells us that God loves us, it is only telling us something that is a fact. It would not be in the Bible if it had not been already known to be a fact.

It was a great discovery for me when I grasped this idea. It seemed to take all of the uncertainty and speculation out of the salvation of the Lord Jesus Christ. It made all that is written concerning Him to be simply a statement of incontrovertible facts.

These are facts we can believe. What is more, we do believe them, as soon as we see that they are facts. We cannot depend upon inward revelations, but anyone can believe the thing that is written. Although this may seem very dry to start with, if continued, it will result in glorious inward revelations. Eventually, we will be led into such a knowledge of God that our lives will be transformed.

This kind of knowing brings us convictions. Convictions are far superior to any inward revelations, delightful though they are. An inward revelation may be upset by the state of one's health or by many other circumstances, but a conviction is permanent. Convince a man that two and two makes four, and no amount of indigestion, influenza, hurricane winds, or anything else but actual lunacy can upset his conviction. He knows addition just as well when he has an attack of indigestion as he knows it when his stomach is in good working order. Convictions come from knowledge. No amount of good feelings or bad feelings, or of good health or bad health, can change knowledge.

Perfect Peace And Comfort

I am absolutely certain that coming to know Him as He is will bring unfailing comfort and peace to every troubled heart. One of Job's friends said in his arguments against Job's bitter complaints, "Acquaint now thyself with him, and be at peace" (Job 22:21). Our Lord, in His last recorded prayer, said, "And this is life eternal, that they might know thee, the only true God, and Jesus Christ whom thou hast sent" (John 17:3). It is not a question of acquaintance with ourselves or of knowing what we are or what we do or what we feel. It is only a question of becoming acquainted

13

with God and getting to know what He is and what He does and what He feels.

Comfort and peace can never come from anything we know about ourselves, but only and always from what we know about Him. We may spend our days in religious service and fill our devotions with fervor and still be miserable. Nothing can set our hearts at rest but acquaintance with God. After all, everything in our salvation depends upon Him.

If we were planning to take a dangerous voyage, our first concern would be about the sort of Captain we were to have. Our common sense would tell us that if the Captain were untrustworthy, no amount of trustworthiness on our part would make our voyage safe. It would be his character, not our own, that would be of paramount importance to us.

I desire to lift some troubled hearts out of their sad and uncomfortable religious lives into the Kingdom of love, joy, and peace, which is their undisputed inheritance. If I manage this, I will feel that my objective in writing this book has been accomplished. I will be able to say, "Lord, now let Your servant depart in peace, for my eyes have seen Your salvation; and my pen has tried to tell it."

It must, however, be clearly understood that my book does not propose to touch on the critical or the theological aspects of our religion. Other and far abler minds can deal with these matters. My book is written for people who, like myself, believe in the Lord Jesus Christ, and who accept the Bible simply as the revelation of Himself.

Leaving aside all critical questions, therefore, I seek only to tell such believers of what seems to me the necessary result of their belief and how they can personally realize it.

There may be mistakes in the telling, and for these I ask the forgiveness of my readers. Nevertheless, the thing I want to say in such a way that no one can fail to understand it is this: our religious lives should be full of joy, peace, and comfort. If we become better acquainted with God, we will experience all that He has for us.

Chapter 2

WHAT IS HIS NAME?

"And Moses said unto God, Behold, when I come unto the children of Israel, and shall say unto them, The God of your fathers hath sent me unto you; and they shall say to me, What is his name? what shall I say unto them?"—Exodus 3:13.

The question of all ages and of every human heart is expressed here—"What is His name?" The fate of humanity hangs on the answer to this question.

As we all know, the condition of a country depends upon the character of its rulers. The state of an army depends upon the officers who command it. And the more absolute the government, the more this is the case.

We can see how it must be, therefore, that everything in the universe depends upon the sort of Creator and Ruler who has brought that universe into existence. The whole welfare of human beings is bound up with the character of their

Creator. If the God who created us is a good God, then everything must be all right for us. After all, a good God cannot ordain anything but good. But if He is a bad God, a careless God, or an unkind God, then we cannot be sure that anything is right. We can have no peace or comfort anywhere.

The true ground for peace and comfort is only to be found in the sort of God we have. Therefore, we need first of all to find out what is His name, or in other words, what is His character—in short, what sort of God He is.

In Bible language, name always means character. Names were not given arbitrarily, but always referred to the character or work of the person named. Cruden, in his Concordance, says that the names of God signify what He really is. The names of God express His attributes, His purposes, His glory, His grace, His mercy, and His love. They express His wisdom, power, and goodness. A careful study of His names will make this plain.

When the children of Israel asked, "What is His name?" they meant, "Who and what is this God of whom you speak? What is His character, what are His attributes, what does He do? What sort of a Being is He?"

The psalmist said, "And they that know thy name will put their trust in thee: for thou, Lord, hast not forsaken them that seek thee" (Psalm 9:10). The writer of Proverbs echos his confidence: "The name of the Lord is a strong tower:

the righteous runneth into it and is safe" (Proverbs 18:10).

"They that know thy name will put their trust in thee." They cannot do anything else, because in knowing His name, they know His character and His nature. They know that He is a God who may be safely trusted to the uttermost.

Trusting The Great I AM

"Some trust in chariots, and some in horses: but we will remember the name of the Lord our God. They are brought down and are fallen: but we are risen, and stand upright" (Psalm 20:7-8). In all that we read concerning Israel of old, we find this constant refrain. All they were and all they had depended upon the fact that their God was the Lord.

"O Lord, there is none like thee, neither is there any God beside thee, according to all that we have heard with our ears. And what one nation in the earth is like thy people Israel, whom God went to redeem to be his own people, to make thee a name of greatness and terribleness, by driving out nations from before thy people, whom thou hast redeemed out of Egypt? For thy people Israel didst thou make thine own people for ever; and thou, Lord, becamest their God" (1 Chronicles 17:20-22). "Happy is that people, that is in such a case: yea, happy is that people, whose God is the Lord" (Psalm 144:15).

Blessed is that nation, happy is that people

whose God is the Lord! All the blessing and happiness of Israel arose from the fact that their God was the Lord. Nothing else was of sufficient importance to be mentioned in the review of their advantages. The fact that their God was the Lord Jehovah was enough to account for every good thing they possessed.

The question of all questions remains, "What is His name?" God Himself answered this question for the Israelites. "And God said unto Moses, I AM THAT I AM: and he said, thus shalt thou say unto the children of Israel, I AM hath sent me unto you. And God said moreover unto Moses, Thus shalt thou say unto the children of Israel, The Lord God of your fathers, the God of Abraham, the God of Isaac, and the God of Jacob, hath sent me unto you: this is my name forever, and this is my memorial unto all generations" (Exodus 3:14-15).

In the gospel of John, Christ adopts this name of "I AM" as His own. When the Jews were questioning Him concerning His authority, "Jesus said unto them, Verily, verily, I say unto you, Before Abraham was, I AM" (John 8:58). In the book of Revelation, He again declares, "I am Alpha and Omega, the beginning and the ending, saith the Lord, which is, and which was, and which is to come, the Almighty" (Revelation 1:8).

These simple words "I am " express God's eternal and unchanging existence. This is the first element necessary in a God who is to be depended upon. No dependence could be placed by any one of us upon a changeable God. He must be the same yesterday, today, and forever, if we are to have any peace or comfort.

Complete Provision

But is this all His name implies, simply *I am*? I am, what?—we ask. What does this *I am* include? It includes everything the human heart longs for and needs.

This unfinished name of God is like a blank check signed by a rich friend. It is given to us to be filled up with whatever sum we desire. The whole Bible tells us what it means. Every attribute of God, every revelation of His character, every proof of His undying love, every declaration of His watchful care, every assertion of His purposes of tender mercy, every manifestation of His loving-kindness, all, are the filling out of this unfinished *I am*.

God tells us through all the pages of His Book what He is. *I am* all that My people need: *I am* their strength; *I am* their wisdom; *I am* their righteousness; *I am* their peace; *I am* their salvation; *I am* their life; *I am* their all in all.

This apparently unfinished name, therefore, is the most comforting name the heart of man could devise. It allows us to add to it, without any limitation, whatever we feel the need of, even "exceeding abundantly above all that we ask or think" (Ephesians 3:20).

But if our hearts are full of our own wretched "I

am's," we will have no ears to hear His glorious, soul-satisfying *I AM*. We say, "Alas, I am such a poor weak creature" or "I am so foolish" or "I am so good-for-nothing" or "I am so helpless." We give these pitiful "I am's" of ours as the reason of the wretchedness and discomfort of our lives. We even feel that we are to be pitied that things are so hard for us. All the while, we entirely ignore the blank check of God's magnificent *I AM* which authorizes us to draw upon Him for an abundant supply for every need.

If you are an uncomfortable Christian, the only thing that will give you a thoroughly comfortable Christian life is to know God. The psalmist says that they that know God's name will put their trust in Him. It is impossible for anyone to know Him and not to trust Him. A trustworthy person commands trust, not by ordering people to trust him, but by winning their trust with his trustworthiness.

What our Lord declares is eternally true, "And I, if I be lifted up, will draw all men unto me" (John 12:32). Once you know Him, Christ is absolutely irresistible. You can no more help trusting Him than you can help breathing. If the whole world would know Him as He is, sinners would fall at His feet in adoring worship. They simply could not help it. His surpassing loveliness would overwhelm them completely.

21

How can we become acquainted with God? There are two things necessary: first, God must reveal Himself; and second, we must accept His revelation and believe what He reveals.

The apostle John tells us, "No man hath seen God at any time; but the only begotten Son, which is in the bosom of the Father, he hath declared him" (John 1:18). Christ, then, is the revelation of God. None of us have seen God, and we never can see Him in this present stage of our existence. But He has incarnated Himself in Christ, and we can see Christ since He was a man like us.

A man who wants to talk with ants might stand over an ant hill and lecture for a whole day. Not one word would reach the ears of the ants. They would run to and fro, utterly unconscious of his presence. But if a man could become an ant, he could live among them and communicate with them.

Incarnation is always necessary when a higher form of life desires to communicate with a lower form. Christ revealed God by what He was, by what He did, and by what He said. From the cradle to the grave, every moment of His life was a revelation of God. We must go to Him then for our knowledge of God. We must refuse to believe anything concerning God that is not revealed to us in Christ. All other revelations are partial and therefore not wholly true. Only in Christ do we see God as He is, for Christ is declared to be the express image of God. (See Hebrews 1:3.)

Christ said and did exactly what God would have under the same circumstances. "I can of mine own self do nothing" (John 5:30) was His continual assertion. "I speak not of myself: but the Father that dwelleth in me, he doeth the works" (John 14:10). "I and my Father are one" (John 10:30). "He that hath seen me hath seen the Father" (John 14:9).

The Bible tells us plainly that in order to know God, we have to look at Christ. We must receive the testimony of Christ.

We are assured that God and Christ are one. When the Jews came to Christ as He was walking in the porch of Solomon's temple and asked Him to tell them plainly who He was, He answered, "I and my Father are one" (John 10:30).

At His last supper with His disciples, He said in answer to their questions, "If ye had known me, ye should have known my Father also: and from henceforth ye know him, and have seen him." But Philip could not understand this and said, "Lord, shew us the Father, and it sufficeth us." And then Jesus repeated His former statement even more strongly, "Have I been so long time with you, and yet hast thou not known me, Philip? he that hath seen me hath seen the Father; and how sayest thou then, Shew us the Father?" (John 14:7-9).

Nothing is more emphatically stated in the New Testament than that we are to behold the "light of the knowledge of the glory of God in the face of Jesus Christ" (2 Corinthians 4:6). We can behold it fully nowhere else.

If we would know the length and breadth and height and depth of what God meant when He gave to Moses that apparently unfinished name of "I AM," we will find it revealed in Christ. He alone is the translation and the image of the invisible God.

It is evident, therefore, that we must never accept any conception of God that is contrary to what we see in Christ. We must reject any view of His character or of His acts or any statement of His relationship with us, no matter how strongly upheld, which differs with what Christ has revealed.

We are all aware that the Old Testament revelation of God sometimes seems to contradict the revelation in Christ. The question arises as to which we are to receive as the truth. God Himself tells us that in these last days He has spoken to us by His Son, who is the "brightness of his glory, and the express image of his person" (Hebrews 1:3). We dare not reject Christ's testimony. But we must look upon the Old Testament revelation, where it differs from the revelation in Christ, as partial and imperfect. We must accept as a true representation of God only that which we find in Christ.

Christ alone tells us the true and genuine name of God. In His last wonderful prayer He says, "I have manifested thy name unto the men which thou gavest me out of the world. . .they have known that all things whatsoever thou hast given me are of thee. For I have given unto them the words which thou gavest me; and they have received them, and have known surely that I came out from thee, and they have believed that thou didst send me" (John 17:6-8). Could we ask for greater authority than this?

Perfect Expression Of God

In the life of Christ, nothing is plainer or more emphatic than His claim that He is a full and complete manifestation of God. In John 14:10, Jesus assures His disciples "the words that I speak unto you I speak not of myself: but the Father that dwelleth in me, he doeth the works." He said only what the Father told Him to say.

The apostle Paul declares that it pleased the Father that "in him dwelleth all the fullness of the Godhead bodily" (Colossians 2:9). We may not understand all that this means theologically. But we at least can see that if we want to know God, we need only to become acquainted with Christ's ways and Christ's character. "He that hath seen me hath seen the Father" (John 14:9). He declares that "neither knoweth any man the Father, save the Son, and he to whomsoever the Son will reveal him" (Matthew 11:27).

This settles it beyond the possibility of argument. We may, and we do, have all sorts of thoughts of God. We may conjecture this or imagine that, but we are wasting our energy. We simply cannot know Him, no man can, except through the revelation of Christ.

We may know many things about Him, but that is very different from knowing Him as He truly is in nature and character. Witnesses have told us of His visible acts, but from these we often get very wrong impressions of His true character. No other witness but Christ can tell us the real secrets of God's heart. Christ is "the only begotten Son, which is in the bosom of the Father, he hath declared him" (John 1:18).

It will make all the difference between comfort and discomfort in our Christian lives if we believe this to be true. If we do believe, then the stern Judge and hard Taskmaster whom we have feared will disappear. His place will be taken by the God of love who is revealed to us in Jesus Christ. He is the God who cares for us as He cares for the sparrows and for the flowers of the field. He even numbers the hairs of our head. No human being could be afraid of a God like this.

If we have been accustomed to approach God with any mistrust of the kindness of His feelings toward us; if our faith has been poisoned by fear; if unworthy thoughts of His character and will have filled our hearts with suspicion of His goodness; if we have pictured Him as an unjust despot or a self-seeking tyrant; if, in short, we have imagined Him in ways other than that which have been revealed to us in Jesus Christ, then we must go back in all simplicity of heart to the records of that lovely life lived in human flesh among men. We must bring our conceptions of God into perfect harmony with the character and ways of Him who declares that He came to manifest the name of God to men.

In reply to the question, "What is His name?" I have only one thing to say: "Ask Christ." We are told He was God manifest in the flesh and that whoever sees Him sees the God who sent Him. It is obvious that, if we want to know the name, we have only to read the manifestation.

This means that we must study the life and words and ways of Christ. We must realize that he that sees Christ sees God. Christ was on earth what God is in heaven. All the darkness that hides the character of God will vanish if we accept the light Christ has shed on the matter. We must believe the manifestation of His name that Christ has given us and refuse to believe anything else.

Heavenly Things Revealed

Nicodemus came to Jesus one night to ask Him how the things He was saying could possibly be true. Jesus told him that whether he understood them or not, they still were true. Jesus then said, "Verily, verily, I say unto thee, We speak that we do know, and testify that we have seen" (John 3:11).

No one who believes in Christ can doubt that He knew God; and no one can question whether or not we should receive His testimony. He knew what He was talking about. What He said is to be received as the absolute truth. He had come down from heaven, and therefore knew about heavenly things.

None of us would dare openly question the truth of this. Yet, a great many of God's children ignore Christ's testimony and choose instead to listen to the testimony of their own doubting hearts. Their hearts tell them that it is impossible for God to be as loving in His care for us or as tender toward our weakness and foolishness or as ready to forgive our sins, as Christ has revealed Him to be.

It must be emphasized that the name, or in other words, the character of His Father which Christ gave, must be His real name and character. He declares of Himself that He was a living manifestation of the Father. In all He said and did, He assures us that it was exactly what the Father would have said and done had He acted directly from His heavenly throne.

In the face of such unqualified assertions from the lips of our Lord Himself, we discover not only our privilege but our duty in Him. We have no choice but to cast out of our conception of God every element that conflicts with the blessed life and character and teaching of Christ. If we want to know the real name of God, we must accept the name Christ has revealed to us. Then we must listen to no other.

The characteristics we see in Christ are the filling out of the "I AM" of God. As we look at the life of Christ and listen to His words, we can hear God saying, "I am rest for the weary; I am peace for the storm-tossed; I am strength for the exhausted; I am wisdom for the foolish; I am righteousness for the sinful; I am all that the neediest soul on earth can want; I am exceeding abundantly, beyond all you can ask or think, of blessing, help, and care."

The doubter may say, "Ah yes, this is no doubt all true, but how can I get hold of it? I am such a poor, unworthy creature that I dare not believe such a fullness of grace can belong to me."

You cannot get hold of it all, but you can let it get hold of you. There is a piece of magnificient good news declared to you in the Bible. You only need to do exactly what you would do when any earthly good news is told you by a reliable source. If the speaker is trustworthy, you believe what he says and act in accordance. You must do the same here. If Christ is trustworthy when He tells you that He is the manifestation of God, you must believe what He says and act accordingly.

You must take your stand on His trustworthiness. You must affirm "I am going to believe what Christ says about God. No matter what things seem to be or what my own thoughts and feelings are or what anybody else may say, I know that what Christ says about God must be true. I am going to believe Him straight through, come what may. He says that He was one with God, so all that He was, God is.

"I will never be frightened of God anymore. I will never again let myself think of Him as a stern Lawgiver who is angry with me because of my sins. I will not view Him as a hard Taskmaster who demands from me impossible tasks. He is not a far-off, unapproachable Deity who is wrapped up in His own glory and is indifferent to my sorrows and my fears. All such ideas of God have become impossible to accept now that I know that Christ is the true manifestation of God."

We can take our stand on this: Christ and God are one. Then we will definitely and unwaveringly refuse to cherish any thought of God that varies with what Christ has revealed. Life will be transformed for us.

We may often have to be fiercely determined to hold steadfastly here. Our old doubts and fears will be sure to come back and demand entrance. But we must turn our backs on them resolutely and declare that we know the name and the character of our God. We know that such things would be impossible to Him. Therefore, we simply refuse to listen for even a moment to any such slander of His character or His ways.

It is unthinkable to suppose that when God told Moses His name was "I AM," that He meant to say, "I am a stern Lawgiver" or "I am a hard Taskmaster." He surely did not mean, "I am a God who is wrapped up in My own glory and am indifferent to the sorrows or the fears of My people." If we try to fill up the blank check of His "I AM" with such things as these, all Christians would be horrified. But do not the doubts and fears of some of these same Christians say exactly these things?

May God grant that we will learn about His true character as we consider the names of God. May our true knowledge of Him make all doubts and fears impossible to us, now and forever.

Chapter 3

THE GOD OF ALL COMFORT

"Blessed be God, even the Father of our Lord Jesus Christ, the Father of mercies, and the God of all comfort; Who comforteth us in all our tribulation, that we may be able to comfort them which are in any trouble, by the comfort wherewith we ourselves are comforted of God"—2 Corinthians 1:3-4.

Among all the names that reveal God, the *God of all comfort* is one of the most lovely and the most absolutely comforting. The words *all comfort* admit no limitations and no deductions. No matter how full of discomforts the outward life of a follower of such a God might be, his spiritual life must be always, and under all circumstances, a comfortable life.

Unfortunately, it often seems as if exactly the opposite were true. The spiritual lives of large numbers of the children of God are full of the utmost discomfort. This discomfort arises from anxiety concerning their relationship to God and doubts of His love. They torment themselves with the thought that they are too good-for-nothing to be worthy of His care. They suspect Him of being indifferent to their trials and of forsaking them in times of need. They are anxious and troubled about everything in their Christian life, about their feelings, their indifference to the Bible, their lack of fervency in prayer, and their coldness of heart. They are tormented with regrets over their past and anxieties for their future. They feel unworthy to enter God's presence, and they dare not believe that they belong to Him.

They can be happy and comfortable with their earthly friends, but they cannot be happy or comfortable with God. Although He declares Himself to be the God of all comfort, they continually complain that they cannot find comfort anywhere. Their sorrowful looks and the mournful tones of their voice show that they are speaking the truth.

Such Christians profess to be the followers of the God of all comfort. But they spread gloom and discomfort wherever they go. It is out of the question for them to hope that they can encourage anyone else to believe in this beautiful name by which He has announced Himself. They cannot show that it is anything more than a pious phrase, which in reality means nothing at all. The obviously uncomfortable religious lives of so many Christians is responsible for much of the unbelief of the world.

The apostle Paul says, "Ye are our epistle written in our hearts, known and read of all men" (2 Corinthians 3:2). What men read in us is far more important to the spread of Christ's Kingdom than we even begin to realize. It is not what we say that witnesses to others, but what we are.

It is easy enough to say a great many beautiful things about God being the God of all comfort. But unless we know what it is to be truly comforted ourselves, we might as well talk to the wind. People must read in our lives what they hear in our words, or all our preaching is worse than useless. We should ask ourselves what they are reading in us. Is it comfort or discomfort that voices itself in our daily lives?

But what is meant by the comfort that God gives? Is it a sort of pious grace that prepares us for heaven but is somehow unfit to bear the brunt of our everyday life with its trials and its pains? Or is it an honest and genuine comfort that enfolds life's trials and pains in an all-embracing peace? With all my heart, I believe it is the latter.

A Picture Of Comfort

None of us cares for pious phrases. We want reality. The reality of being comforted and comfortable is almost more delightful than any other thing in life. A thousand times in our lives, we have said, with a sigh of relief as burdens are laid down, "Well, this *is* comfortable." In that word, *comfortable*, there has been comprised more of rest, relief, satisfaction, and pleasure than any other word in the English language. We cannot fail, therefore, to understand the meaning of this name of God—the God of all comfort.

But alas, we have failed to believe it. The joy and delight of it is more than our poor, suspicious natures can take in. We may venture to hope sometimes that little scraps of comfort may be granted to us. But we run away frightened at the thought of the *all comfort* that is ours in the salvation of the Lord Jesus Christ.

Yet, what more could He have said about it than this—"As one whom his mother comforteth, so will I comfort you; and ye shall be comforted" (Isaiah 66:13). Notice the *as* and *so* in this passage—*as* one whom his mother comforteth, *so* will I comfort you. It is true comforting that is meant here—the sort of comforting that the child feels when he is held close to his mother's heart.

How many of us have honestly believed that God's comfort is actually as tender and true as a mother's comfort. Instead of thinking of ourselves as being held on His knees and hugged to His heart, we tend to look upon Him as a stern, unbending Judge. We see Him holding us at a distance, demanding our respectful homage, and being critical of our slightest faults. Is it any wonder that our faith, instead of making us comfortable, has made us thoroughly uncomfortable? Who could help being uncomfortable in the presence of such a Judge?

I rejoice to say that the stern Judge is not there! He does not exist. The God who does exist is a God who is like a mother. He says to us plainly, "As one whom his mother comforteth, so will I comfort you."

"I, even I, am he that comforteth you" (Isaiah 51:12), God says to the poor, frightened children of Israel. And then He reproaches them for not being comforted. Why should you let anything make you afraid when here is the Lord, your Maker, ready and longing to comfort you. "And forgettest the Lord thy maker, that hath stretched forth the heavens, and laid the foundations of the earth; and hast feared continually every day because of the fury of oppressor, as if he were ready to destroy? and where is the fury of the oppressor?" (Isaiah 51:13).

The God who exists is the God and Father of our Lord Jesus Christ. He is the God who so loved the world that He sent His Son, not to judge the world, but to save it. He is the God who anointed the Lord Jesus Christ to bind up the broken-hearted and to proclaim liberty to the captives and the opening of the prison to them that are bound and to comfort *all* that mourn.

Every captive of sin, every prisoner in infirmity, every mourning heart throughout the whole world must be included in this *all*. It would not be *all* if there was one single one left out, no matter how insignificant, unworthy, or even how feeble-minded that one might be. The ones who need comfort most are the ones that our God, like a mother, wants to comfort.

This is the glory of a religion of love. And this is the glory of faith in the Lord Jesus Christ. He was anointed to comfort *all that mourn.* The *God of all comfort* sent His Son to be the comforter of a mourning world. All through His life on earth, He fulfilled His divine mission.

When His disciples asked Him to call down fire from heaven to consume some people who refused to receive Him, "He turned and rebuked them, and said, Ye know not what manner of spirit ye are of. For the Son of man is not come to destroy men's lives, but to save them" (Luke 10:55-56).

He received sinners and ate with them. He welcomed Mary Magdalene when all men turned from her. He even refused to condemn the woman who was taken in the very act of sin, but said to the Scribes and Pharisees who had brought her before Him, "He that is without sin among you, let him first cast a stone at her" (John 8:7). Convicted by their own consciences, they all went out one by one without condemning her. He then said to her, "Neither do I condemn thee: go, and sin no more" (John 8:11).

No Room For Doubt

Two little girls were talking about God, and one said, "I know God does not love me. He could not care for such a tiny little girl like me."

37

"Dear me, Sis," said the other girl, "don't you know that is just what God is for—to take care of tiny little girls who can't take care of themselves, just like us."

"Is He?" said the first little girl. "I did not know that. Then I don't need to worry anymore, do I?"

This is just what the Lord Jesus Christ is for—to care for and comfort *all* who mourn. Remember, it would not be *all* if you were left out. You may be so depressed that you can hardly lift up your head; but Paul tells us that our God is the "God that comforteth those that are cast down" (2 Corinthians 7:6). If you are cast down, you can claim the comforting of Christ. This mission of comfort is greatly needed in a world of mourning like ours. Every sorrowful heart may be comforted with this comforting of God.

Our Comforter is not far off in heaven where we cannot find Him. He is close at hand. He abides with us. When Christ was going away from this earth, He told His disciples, "And I will pray the Father, and he shall give you another Comforter, that he may abide with you for ever. . .But the Comforter, which is the Holy Ghost, whom the Father will send in my name, he shall teach you all things, and bring all things to your remembrance, whatsoever I have said unto you" (John 14:16,26).

Then He declared, as though it was the necessary result of the coming of this divine Comforter, "Peace I leave with you, my peace I give unto you:

not as the world giveth, give I unto you. Let not your heart be troubled, neither let it be afraid" (John 14:27). Oh, how can we, in the face of these tender and loving words, go about with troubled and frightened hearts?

A Comforter—what a word of bliss! If we only could realize all that it means. Let us repeat it to ourselves until its meaning sinks into the very depths of our being. He is an *abiding Comforter*, too, not one who comes and goes and is never on hand when most needed. He is always present and always ready to give us "joy for mourning, and the garment of praise for the spirit of heaviness" (Isaiah 61:3).

I have often wondered whether those early disciples realized what this glorious legacy of a Comforter meant. The majority of the disciples of Christ today do not. If they did, there could not possibly be so many uncomfortable Christians.

Overcoming Faults

You may ask whether this divine Comforter reproves us for our sins. How can we get any comfort out of this? This is one of the places where the comfort comes in. What sort of creatures would we be if we had no divine teacher to show us our faults and awaken the desire to get rid of them?

For example, I may be walking along the street with a gaping hole in the back of my dress. It is certainly a great comfort to me to have a kind friend who will tell me about it. Similarly, it is indeed a comfort to know that there is always abiding with me a divine, all-seeing Comforter. He will reprove me for all my faults, rather than allow me to go on in a fatal unconsciousness of them.

Emerson says that it is far better for a man to see his own faults, rather than for anyone else to see them. A moment's thought will convince us that this is true. We will be thankful for the Comforter who reveals our faults to us.

I remember the comfort it was for me to have a sister who always knew the proper thing to do. When we went out together, she always kept me in order. I never felt any anxiety or responsibility about myself if she was near. I knew she would keep a strict watch over me and nudge me or whisper to me if I was making any mistakes. I was always made comfortable, rather than uncomfortable, in her presence. But when I went anywhere alone, I would indeed feel uncomfortable. Then there was no one standing by to keep me straight.

Despite Our Unworthiness

"For the Lord shall comfort Zion: he will comfort all her waste places; and he will make her wilderness like Eden, and her desert like a garden of the Lord; joy and gladness shall be found therein, thanksgiving, and the voice of melody" (Isaiah 51:3).

You may object, perhaps, that you are not worthy of His comforts. I do not suppose you are. No one ever is. But you need His comforting all the more because you are not worthy. Christ came into the world to save sinners, not those who thought they were good. Your unworthiness is your greatest claim for His salvation.

In the same passage in Isaiah in which He tells us that He has seen our ways and is angry with us, He assures us that He will heal us and restore comfort to us. Anger in this sense means the anger that love always feels with any fault in those it loves. He restores comfort to us. He does it by revealing our sin and healing it.

The avenue to the consolation of the divine Comforter lies in the need of comfort. This explains the reason why the Lord often allows us to experience sorrow and trials. "Therefore, behold, I will allure her, and bring her into the wilderness, and speak comfortably unto her" (Hosea 2:14).

We may be in a wilderness of disappointment and suffering. We wonder why the God who loves us allowed it. But He knows that it is only in the wilderness that we can hear and receive the comforting words He has to pour out upon us. We must feel the need of comfort before we can listen to the words of comfort.

God knows that it is better for us to need His comfort and receive it, than for us not to need it and be without it. The consolation of God means substituting a far higher and better thing than what we lose to get it. The things we lose are earthly things. Those He substitutes are heavenly.

Who would not be thankfully drawn by our God into any earthly wilderness if there we find the unspeakable joys of union with Him. Paul could say, "Yea, doubtless and I count all things but loss for the excellency of the knowledge of Christ Jesus my Lord: for whom I have suffered the loss of all things, and do count them but dung, that I might win Christ" (Philippians 3:8). If we have even the faintest glimpse of what winning Christ means, we will say the same.

Believing The Word

Strangely enough, it is often easy for us to believe that our God is the God of all comfort when we are happy and do not need comforting. As soon as we are in trouble and need, however, it seems impossible to believe that there can be any comfort for us anywhere. It is as if, in our reading of the Bible, we reversed its meaning. Instead of "Blessed are they that mourn: for they shall be comforted" (Matthew 5:4), we read "Blessed are they that rejoice, for they, and they only, shall be comforted." We almost unconsciously alter the Bible words a little, and so make the meaning exactly opposite to what it actually is. Or we may put in so many "ifs" and "buts" that we take the whole point out of what is said.

Take, for instance, those beautiful words, "God, that comforteth those that are cast down" (2 Corinthians 7:6). Have we ever been tempted to make it read in our secret hearts, "God who for-saketh those who are cast down;" or perhaps, "God who overlooks those who are cast down;" or, "God who will comfort those who are cast down if they show themselves worthy of comfort." Consequently, instead of being comforted, we have been plunged into misery and despair.

The psalmist tells us that God will "comfort me on every side" (Psalm 71:21). What an all-embracing bit of comfort this is! *On every side,* with no aching spot to be left uncomforted. And yet, in times of trial, how many Christians secretly read this as though it said, "God will comfort us on every side, except the side where our trials lie; on that side there is no comfort anywhere." But God says *every side,* and it is only unbelief on our part that leads us to make an exception of our side with trials.

Like Israel of old we have difficulty believing and accepting God's comfort. On one side God said to Zion, "Sing, O heavens; and be joyful, O earth; and break forth into singing, O mountains: for the Lord hath comforted his people, and will have mercy upon his afflicted. But Zion said, The Lord hath forsaken me, and my Lord hath forgotten me" (Isaiah 49:13-14).

Then God's answer came in those wonderful words, full of enough comfort to meet the needs of all the sorrows of all humanity: "Can a woman forget her sucking child, that she should not have compassion on the son of her womb? yea, they

43

may forget, yet will I not forget thee. Behold, I have graven thee upon the palms of my hands; thy walls are continually before me" (Isaiah 49:15-16).

Receiving God's Comfort

You may ask how you are to get hold this divine comfort. My answer is that you must take it. God's comfort is being continually and abundantly given, but unless you will accept it, you cannot have it.

Divine comfort does not come to us in any mysterious or arbitrary way. It comes as the result of a divine method. The indwelling Comforter brings to our remembrance comforting things concerning our Lord. If we believe them, we are comforted by them.

We are reminded of a Scripture text or the verse of a hymn or some thought concerning the love of Christ and His tender care for us. If we receive the suggestion in simple faith, we cannot help being comforted. But we may refuse to listen to the voice of our Comforter and insist instead on listening to the voice of discouragment or despair. When that happens, no comfort can possibly reach our souls.

Even a mother may lavish all motherly comfort on a weeping child in vain. The child sits up stiff and sullen and refuses to be comforted. All her comforting words fall on unbelieving ears. To be comforted by comforting words, we must believe these words.

God has spoken enough comforting words to comfort a whole universe. Yet, we see all around us unhappy Christians, worried Christians, and gloomy Christians. It seems that not one of these comforting words is allowed to enter their hearts. A great many Christians actually think it is wrong to be comforted. They feel too unworthy. If any ray of comfort steals into their hearts, they sternly shut it out. Like Rachel, Jacob, and the psalmist, their souls refuse to be comforted.

Paul tells us, "Whatsoever things were written aforetime were written for our learning, that we through patience and comfort of the scriptures might have hope" (Romans 15:4). But if we are to be comforted by the Scriptures, we must first believe them. Nothing that God has said can possibly comfort a person who does not believe it to be true.

When the captain of a vessel tells us that his vessel is safe, we must first believe him before we can feel comfortable on board that vessel. When the guard on a railway tells us we are on the right train, before we can settle down comfortably in our seats, we must trust his word. This is all so self-evident that it might seem foolish to call attention to it. But in religious matters, the self-evident truths are often the ones most easily overlooked.

I have known people who insisted on realizing

God's comfort while still doubting His words of comfort. They even thought they could not believe His comforting words at all until they had first felt the comfort in their own souls! The passenger on the railway might as well insist on having a feeling of comfortable assurance that he is on the right train, before he could make up his mind to believe the word of the guard. Always and in everything, comfort must follow faith. It can never precede it.

This matter of comfort is exactly the same as every other experience in the Christian life. God says, "Believe, and then you can feel." We say, "Feel, and then we can believe." God's order is not arbitrary. It exists in the very nature of things.

In all earthly matters, we recognize this. We are never so foolish to expect to feel we have anything, until we first believe that it is in our possession. I could not possibly feel glad that I had a fortune in the bank, unless I knew that it was really there. But in spiritual things we reverse God's order (which is the order of nature as well). We refuse to believe that we possess anything until we first feel as if we had it.

Let me illustrate. We are, let us suppose, overwhelmed with cares and anxieties. It often happens in this world. To comfort us in these circumstances the Lord assures us that we need not be anxious about anything. We may commit all our cares to Him, for He cares for us. We are all familiar with the passage where He tells us to behold the fowls of the air and to consider the lilies of the fields. He assures us that we are of much more value than they, and that, if He cares for them, He will much more care for us. (See Matthew 6:26-30.)

One would think there was enough comfort here for every care or sorrow all the world over. God takes our cares and our burdens and carries them for us. The Almighty God, the Creator of heaven and earth, controls everything and forsees everything. He can manage everything in the best possible way. He declares that He will take care of us. What could possibly be a greater comfort? And yet, how few people are comforted by it.

Why is this? Simply because they do not believe it. They are waiting to have an inward feeling that His words are true before they will believe them. They look upon them as beautiful things for Him to say. They wish they could believe them. But they do not think they can be true in their own special case, unless they can have an inward *feeling* that they are. Therefore, they do not expect Him to care for their affairs at all. "Oh, if I could only *feel* it was all true," we say; and God says, "Oh, if you would only *believe* it is all true!"

Prescription For Comfort

The remedy for this is plain. If we want to be comforted, we must make up our minds to believe every word of comfort God has ever spoken. We must refuse to listen to any words of discomfort spoken by our own hearts or by our circumstances. We must be stubborn in our belief, in spite of every sorrow and trial. Then we can accept and rejoice in His all-embracing comfort.

When everything around us seems out of sorts, it is not always easy to believe God's words of comfort. We must put our will into this matter of being comforted, just as we have to put our wills into all other matters in our spiritual life. We must choose to be comforted.

It may seem impossible when things look all wrong to believe that God can be caring for us as a mother cares for her children. We know perfectly well that He says He does care for us in this tender and loving way. Yet we say, "Oh, if I could only believe that, of course I would be comforted."

Here is where our will must come in. We *must* believe it. We must say to ourselves, "God says it and it is true and I am going to believe it, no matter how it looks." Then we must never permit ourselves to doubt or question it again. Whoever will adopt this plan will come, sooner or later, into a place of abounding comfort.

The psalmist says, "In the multitude of my thoughts within me thy comforts delight my soul" (Psalm 94:19). Among the multitude of our thoughts within us, there are far too many thoughts of our own discomforts, rather than of God's comforts. We must think of His comforts if we are to be comforted by them. It might be a good exercise for some of us to analyze our thoughts for a few days. We could see how many thoughts we actually do give to God's comforts, compared to the number we give to our own discomforts. I think the result would amaze us!

If people are to think on the comfort of God, the preachers of the gospel must consider what they are called to preach. The true commission, in my opinion, is found in Isaiah 40:1-2, "Comfort ye, comfort ye my people, saith your God. Speak ye comfortably to Jerusalem, and cry unto her, that her warfare is accomplished, that her iniquity is pardoned: for she hath received of the Lord's hands double for all her sins."

"Comfort ye my people" is the divine command. If you feel called to preach the gospel, see to it that you preach Christ's gospel and not man's. Christ comforts, man scolds. Christ's gospel is always good news. Man's gospel is generally a mixture of a little good news and a great deal of bad news. Even where it tries to be good news, it is so hampered with "ifs" and "buts" and all sorts of man-made conditions that it utterly fails to bring any lasting joy or comfort.

The only gospel that can rightly be called the gospel was proclaimed by the angel to the frightened shepherds who were keeping watch over their flocks by night: "Fear not: for, behold, I bring you good tidings of great joy, which shall be to all people. For unto you is born this day in the city of David, a Saviour, which is Christ the Lord" (Luke 2:10-11).

49

Never were more comfortable words preached to any congregation. If only all the preachers would speak the same comfortable words to their people. Then, if all who hear these words would believe them and take comfort in them, there would be no more uncomfortable Christians. The apostle Paul's prayer for the Thessalonians would be fulfilled. "Now our Lord Jesus Christ himself, and God, even our Father, which hath loved us, and hath given us everlasting consolation and good hope through grace, Comfort your hearts, and stablish you in every good word and work" (2 Thessalonians 2:16-17).

Chapter 4

THE LORD OUR SHEPHERD

"The Lord is my Shepherd; I shall not want"—
Psalm 23:1.

Perhaps no aspect in which the Lord reveals Himself to us is more full of genuine comfort than the one expressed in the Twenty-third Psalm, and in its corresponding passage in the tenth chapter of John's gospel. The psalmist claims that the Lord is my Shepherd. The Lord Himself declares that He is the *Good* Shepherd. Can we conceive of anything more comforting?

The highest and grandest truths of the faith of the Lord Jesus Christ are often written in the simplest and commonest verses in the Bible. We have known those texts from our childhood, when we learned them in the nursery at our mother's knee. They were used by those who loved us to explain, in the simplest possible way, the love of our heavenly Father and the reasons for trusting Him. These texts contain the whole story of salvation in their simple statements.

We need to get back into the nursery and take up those beloved Scriptures from our childhood once more. While reading them with the intelligence of our grown-up years, we need to believe them with all our simple, childlike faith.

Each one of us remembers the Twenty-third Psalm. We can still recall our joy and pride when we were first able to repeat it without mistake. Since then, we have always know it. Its words, perhaps, sound so old and familiar that you cannot see their deep meaning. But in truth, they tell us the whole story of our faith, in words of wondrous depth of meaning. I doubt whether it has entered into the heart of any man to comprehend the things they reveal.

Repeat these familiar words over to yourself afresh: "The Lord is my Shepherd, I shall not want."

Who is it that is your Shepherd?

The Lord! Oh, my friends, what a wonderful announcement! The Lord God of heaven and earth, the Almighty Creator of all things, He who holds the universe in His hand as though it were a very little thing, He is your Shepherd. He has charged Himself with the care of you, as a shepherd is charged with the care of his sheep.

If your heart will only take in this thought, your life will be full of the most profound comfort from now on. All your old uncomfortable religion will drop off forever, as the mist disappears in the blaze of the summer sun.

Comforted By The Shepherd

I experienced the abundant comfort from this Scripture at one time in my Christian life. The Twenty-third Psalm had always been familiar to me from my nursery days, but it had never seemed to have any special meaning. Then came a critical moment in my life when I was sadly in need of comfort. I could not at the moment lay my hands on my Bible. I desperately tried to remember some passage of Scripture that would help me. Immediately there flashed into my mind the words, "The Lord is my Shepherd, I shall not want."

At first I turned from it almost with scorn. "Such a common text as that," I said to myself, "is not likely to do me any good." I tried hard to think of a more uncommon one, but none would come. At last it almost seemed as if there was no other verse in the whole Bible.

Finally I was reduced to saying, "Well, if I cannot think of any other verse, I must try to get what little good I can out of this one." I began to repeat to myself, "The Lord is my Shepherd, I shall not want." Suddenly, as I did so, the words were divinely illuminated. Such floods of comfort poured out upon me that I felt as if I could never have a trouble again.

The moment I could get hold of a Bible, I turned over its pages with eagerness. I needed to see whether such untold treasures of comfort were actually mine. Could I dare to let my heart experience the full enjoyment of them?

I built up a pyramid of declarations and promises concerning the Lord being our Shepherd. Once built, it presented an immoveable and indestructible front to all the winds and storms of doubt or trial that could assail it. And I became convinced, beyond a shadow of doubt, that the Lord truly was my Shepherd. In giving Himself this name, He assumed the duties belonging to the name. Furthermore, He declares "I am the good shepherd: the good shepherd giveth his life for the sheep" (John 10:11).

Jesus Himself draws the contrast between a good shepherd and a bad shepherd. He follows up His announcement, "I am the good shepherd," with the words, "But he that is an hireling, and not the shepherd, whose own the sheep are not, seeth the wolf coming, and leaveth the sheep, and fleeth: and the wolf catcheth them and scattereth the sheep" (John 10:12).

Woe To Faithless Shepherds

Through the mouth of His prophets, the Lord pours down a scathing condemnation upon all faithless shepherds. "And the Lord said unto me, Take unto thee yet the instruments of a foolish shepherd. Woe to the idle shepherd that leaveth the flock! the sword shall be upon his arm, and upon his right eye: his arm shall be clean dried up,

and his right eye shall be utterly darkened"
(Zechariah 11:15,17).

The prophet Ezekiel says, "Thus saith the Lord
God unto the shepherds; Woe be to the shepherds
of Israel that do feed themselves! should not the
shepherds feed the flocks?. . .The diseased have ye
not strengthened, neither have ye healed that
which was sick, neither have ye bound up that
which was broken, neither have ye bought again
that which was driven away, neither have ye
sought that which was lost; but with force and
with cruelty have ye ruled them. . . .Therefore, O
ye shepherds, hear the word of the Lord; Thus
saith the Lord God; Behold, I am against the shepherds; and I will require my flock at their hand,
and cause them to cease from feeding the flock"
(Ezekiel 34:2,4,9-10).

Surely no Christian could ever accuse our divine
Shepherd of being as faithless and unkind as those
He condemns. Yet, although they do not put it
into words and perhaps hardly realize their feel-
ings themselves, some Christians do look upon
Him as a faithless Shepherd.

What else can it mean when Christians complain
that the Lord has forsaken them? They cry to Him
for spiritual food and say that He does not hear.
They are surrounded by enemies, and they claim
that He does not deliver them. When their souls
find themselves in dark places, they insist that He
does not come to their rescue. They cry that when
they are weak, He does not strengthen them. When

they are spiritually sick, they say He does not heal them.

What are all these doubts and discouragements but secret accusations against our good Shepherd? They accuse Him of the very things which He Himself so scathingly condemns.

A dear Christian, who had just discovered what it meant to have the Lord as his Shepherd, said to me, "Of course, I had always known that was what He was called, but it meant nothing to me; and I believe I read the Twenty-third Psalm as though it was written, 'The Lord is the sheep, and I am the shepherd, and, if I do not keep a tight hold on Him, He will run away.' When dark days came, I never for a moment thought that He would stick by me; and when my soul was starving and cried out for food, I never dreamed He would feed me. I see now that I never looked upon Him as a faithful Shepherd at all. But now all is different. I myself am not one bit better or stronger, but I have discovered that I have a good Shepherd, and that is all I need. I see now that it is true that the Lord is my Shepherd, and that I shall not want."

Are you like the Christian who is quoted above? You have said hundreds of times, "The Lord is my Shepherd." But have you ever believed it to be true? Have you felt safe and happy and free from care as a sheep must feel when under the care of a good shepherd? Or have you felt yourself to be like a poor, forlorn sheep without a shepherd? Do you believe that you have an unfaithful, inefficient shepherd who does not supply your needs and leaves you in time of danger and darkness?

Answer this question honestly in your own soul. Have you had a comfortable spiritual life or an uncomfortable one? How can you reconcile an uncomfortable Christian life with the statement that the Lord is your Shepherd, and, therefore, you shall not want? You say that He is your Shepherd. Yet, you complain that you do want. Who has made the mistake—you or the Lord?

Perhaps you will say, "Oh no, I do not blame the Lord, but I am so weak and so foolish and so ignorant that I am not worthy of His care." But do you know that sheep are always weak and helpless and silly? The reason they need to have a shepherd to care for them is because they are unable to care for themselves.

The welfare and safety of sheep does not in the least depend upon their own strength. It does not rely upon their own wisdom or anything in themselves. It rests entirely upon the care of their shepherd. If you are a sheep, your welfare also must depend completely upon your Shepherd and not at all on yourself.

A Story Of Two Flocks

Let us imagine two flocks of sheep meeting at the end of the winter to compare their experiences. One flock is fat and strong and in good condition. The other is poor and lean and diseased.

Will the healthy flock boast of themselves and say, "See what splendid care we have taken of ourselves. What good, strong, and wise sheep we must be." Of course not. Their boasting would all be about their shepherd. "See what a good shepherd we have," they would say, "and how he has cared for us. Through all the storms of the winter, he has protected us and has defended us from every wild beast and has always provided us with the best of food."

Would the poor, wretched, diseased sheep blame themselves and say, "Alas! what wicked sheep we must be, to be in such poor condition!" No, they too would speak only of their shepherd, but how different would be their story. "Alas," they would say, "our shepherd was very different from yours. He fed himself, but he did not feed us. He did not strengthen us when we were weak or heal us when we were sick or bind us up when we were broken or look for us when we were lost. It is true that he stayed by us in clear and pleasant weather, when no enemies were near, but in times of danger or of storm, he abandoned us and fled. Oh, that we had a good shepherd like yours!"

We all understand this responsibility of the shepherd in the case of sheep. But when we transfer the illustration to our faith, we shift all the responsibility from the Shepherd's shoulders and lay it upon the sheep. We demand that the poor human sheep possess the wisdom, care, and power for their provision that can only belong to the divine Shepherd. Of course, the poor human sheep fail. Their spiritual lives become thoroughly uncomfortable and even sometimes miserable.

There is a difference between sheep and us in this. They have neither the intelligence nor the power to withdraw themselves from the care of their shepherd, while we do. We cannot imagine one of them saying, "Oh yes, we have a good shepherd who says he will take care of us, but then we do not feel worthy of his care. Therefore, we are afraid to trust him. He says he has provided for us green pastures and a safe and comfortable fold. But we are such poor, good-for-nothing creatures that we have not dared to enter his fold or feed in his pastures. We have felt it would be presumption. In our humility, we have been trying to do the best we could for ourselves. The strong, healthy sheep may trust themselves to the shepherd's care, but not such miserable half-starved sheep as we are. It is true we have had a very hard time of it and are in a sad and forlorn condition; but then, we are such poor, unworthy creatures that we must expect this and must try to be resigned to it."

Silly as sheep are, we know that no sheep could be so silly as to talk in this way. Yet, we are so much wiser than sheep, in our own estimation, that we think the sort of trust that sheep exercise will not be sufficient for us. In our superior intelligence, we presume to take matters into our own hands and so shut ourselves out from the Shepherd's care.

If any sheep in the flock of Christ find themselves in a poor condition, there are only two explanations possible. Either the Lord is not a good Shepherd and does not care for His sheep, or His sheep have not believed in His care and have been afraid or ashamed to trust themselves to it.

None will dare to say or even think that the Lord can be anything but a good Shepherd. The fault, therefore, must lie here: either you have not believed He was your Shepherd at all, or believing it, you have refused to let Him take care of you.

The Shepherd's Reputation

It is important that you face this matter honestly and give yourself a definite answer. More than your own welfare and comfort depend upon your understanding of this blessed relationship—the glory of your Shepherd is at stake. Have you ever thought of the grief and dishonor this sad condition of yours brings upon Him? The credit of a shepherd depends upon the condition of his flock. He might make a great boast of his qualifications as a shepherd. But it would be an empty claim if His flocks had some missing, some with lean ribs and broken bones, and some in a diseased condition.

If the owner of sheep is thinking of employing a shepherd, he requires a reference from the shepherd's last employer. He wants to learn how his flock fared under the shepherd's care. The Lord makes statements about Himself as the Good Shepherd. He is telling the world and the Church, "I am the Good Shepherd." If they ask, "Where are Your sheep, what condition are they in?" can He point to us as being a credit to His care?

It is a grievous thing if any of us refuse to let the Shepherd take care of us. We would bring discredit upon His name by our forlorn condition. The universe is looking to see what the Lord Jesus Christ is able to make of us and what kind of sheep we are. It wants to see whether we are well-fed, healthy, and happy. Their verdict concerning Him will largely depend upon what they see in us.

Paul wrote to the Ephesians that he had been called to preach to the Gentiles the unsearchable riches of Christ. He earnestly desired to make all men see the fellowship of the mystery which had been hidden in God from the beginning of the world. Then he added the significant words that the object of it all was, "To the intent that now unto principalities and powers in heavenly places might be known by the church the manifold wisdom of God, According to the eternal purpose which he purposed in Christ Jesus our Lord" (Ephesians 3:10-11).

We may be amazed at the thought that God has purposed such a glorious destiny for His sheep. He has made His manifold wisdom known to the universe through what He has done for us! Surely this should make us eager to abandon ourselves to Him in the most absolute trust for salvation to the very uttermost. He may then get great glory in the universe, and the whole world may come to trust Him.

But if we will not let Him save us, if we reject His care and refuse to feed in His pastures or to lie down in His fold, then we will be a starved and shivering flock. We will be sick, wretched, and full of complaints. Furthermore, we will bring dishonor upon Him and, by our forlorn condition, hinder the world from coming to Him.

Bringing Unbelievers Into The Fold

I am not surprised that unbelievers are not drawn into the Church when I contemplate the condition of believers. I do not wonder that in some churches there are no conversions from one end of the year to the other. If I was a poor sheep wandering in the wilderness, and I saw some poor, wretched, sick-looking sheep peeping out of a fold calling me to come in, and if I saw that the fold was hard, bare, and uncomfortable, I would not be tempted to go inside.

Somebody said that some churches are too much like well-ordered graveyards—people are brought in and buried and that is the end of it. Of course, you cannot expect living people to want to make their homes in graveyards. We must have a fold that shows sheep that are in good condition if we expect outsiders to come into that fold. If we want to attract others to the salvation of the Lord Jesus Christ, we must show them that it is a satisfying and comfortable salvation. No one wants to add to their earthly discomforts by getting an uncomfortable religion. It is useless to expect to win outsiders by the sight of our wretchedness.

Surely, if you do not care for yourself, you must care for the dishonor you bring upon your divine Shepherd by your poor and wretched condition. You long to serve Him and to bring Him glory. You can do it if you show the world that He is a Shepherd whom it is safe to trust.

Let me help you to do this. First, realize what a shepherd must be and do in order to be a good shepherd. Next, face the fact that the Lord is truly, in the very highest sense of the word, the Good Shepherd. Then say the words over to yourself with all the will power you can muster, "The Lord is my Shepherd. He is. He is. No matter what I feel, He says He is, and He is. I am going to believe it, come what may." Then repeat the words with a different emphasis each time:

The *Lord* is my Shepherd.

The Lord *is* my Shepherd.

The Lord is *my* Shepherd.

The Lord is my *Shepherd.*

Imagine what your ideal Shepherd would be. Think of all that you would require from anyone filling such a position of trust and responsibility. Then know that an ideal far beyond yours, and a conception of the duties of such a position higher than any you ever dreamed of, was in the mind of our Lord when He said, "I am the Good Shepherd."

He, better than any other, knew the sheep He had to save. He knew a shepherd's duties. He knew that the shepherd is responsible for his flock. He is bound, at any loss of comfort or of health or even of life itself, to care for them and to bring them all home safely to the Master's fold. Therefore, Jesus said, "And this is the Father's will which hath sent me, that of all which he hath given me I should lose nothing, but should raise it up again at the last day" (John 6:39). And again He said, "The good shepherd giveth his life for the sheep." And still again, "My sheep hear my voice, and I know them, and they follow me: And I give unto them eternal life; and they shall never perish, neither shall any man pluck them out of my hand" (John 10:11, 27-28).

Centuries before Jesus came to be the Shepherd, the Father said, "Therefore will I save my flock. . .And I will set up one shepherd over them, and he shall feed them, even my servant David; he shall feed them, and he shall be their shepherd" (Ezekiel 34:22-23).

We catch a glimpse of the Father's yearning love as we read these words. He laid the welfare of the flock upon One who was mighty; therefore, none who are in this flock need to fear any evil.

He has undertaken His duties, knowing perfectly well what the responsibilities are. He knows that He has to deal with very silly sheep, who have no strength to protect themselves. They have no wisdom to guide themselves and nothing impressive about them but their utter helplessness and weakness. But none of these things baffle the Shepherd. His strength and His skill are sufficient to meet every possible emergency.

The Only Hindrance

There is only one thing that can hinder Him: if the sheep will not trust Him or refuse to let Him take care of them. If they stand at a distance, look at the food He has provided and long for it and cry for it but refuse to eat it, He cannot satisfy their hunger. If they linger outside the shelter He has made and are afraid to go in and enjoy it because they feel too distrustful or too unworthy, He cannot protect them. No sheep is so silly as to act in this way. But we human beings, who are so much wiser than sheep, do it continually.

No sheep, if it could talk, would say to the shepherd, "I long for the food you have provided and for the shelter and peace of your fold. I wish I might dare to enjoy them; but, I feel too unworthy! I am too weak and foolish. I do not feel grateful enough. I am afraid I do not feel quite hungry enough or enough in earnest about wanting it. I dare not presume to think you mean all these good things for me."

One can imagine how grieved and wounded a good shepherd would be at a speech as this. Surely our Lord has given us a glimpse into His tender sorrow over those who would not trust Him when He beheld Jerusalem and wept over it saying, "If thou hadst known, even thou, at least in this thy day, the things which belong unto thy peace! but now they are hid from thine eyes" (Luke 19:42).

Dear Christians, have you sometimes grieved and wounded your divine Shepherd by such speeches? If you have, come over on the Shepherd's side of the question. Try to think how He feels and what His thoughts concerning you are. If He is your Shepherd, then He wants to care for you in the very best possible way; for He is a good Shepherd and cares for His sheep. It does not matter what you think about it or how you feel. You are not the Shepherd. You are only the sheep. The important point is what He thinks and how He feels.

Lose sight of yourself for a moment and try to put yourself in the Shepherd's place. Consider your condition as He considers it. See Him coming out to seek you in your far-off wandering. See His tender, yearning love, His unspeakable longing to save you. Believe His own description of Himself, and take Him at His own sweet word.

Simple Trust

The trouble is that our faith is not simple enough to take Him at His word. We feel we must add all sorts of "buts" and "ifs" of our own. We obscure the sunshine of His love with clouds of our own imagining. If we only knew the things which belong to our peace, how quickly we would throw aside every "if" and "but" of unbelief. We would rapturously plunge ourselves headlong into an unquestioning faith in all that He has told us of His almighty and never-failing love and care.

But you may ask, if all this is true of the Shepherd, what is the part of the sheep?

The part of the sheep is very simple. It is only to trust and to follow. The Shepherd does all the rest. He leads the sheep in the right direction. He chooses their paths for them and sees that the sheep can walk in safety. When He sends out His sheep, He goes before them. The sheep have none of the planning to do, none of the decisions to make, none of the foresight or wisdom to exercise. They have absolutely nothing to do but to trust themselves entirely to the care of the good Shepherd and to follow Him wherever He leads.

It is very simple. There is nothing complicated in trusting when the one we are called upon to trust is absolutely trustworthy. There is nothing complicated in obedience when we have perfect confidence in the power we are obeying.

Begin to trust and follow your Shepherd today. Abandon yourself to His care and guidance as a sheep in the care of a shepherd and trust Him completely. You need not be afraid to follow Him wherever He leads, for He always leads His sheep into green pastures and beside still waters. This is true even though you may seem to be in the very midst of a desert, with nothing green about you, inwardly or outwardly.

. You may think you will have to make a long journey before you can get into any green pastures. He has power to make the desert flourish and blossom as the rose. He has promised, "Instead of the thorn shall come up the fir tree, and instead of the briar shall come up the myrtle tree" and "In the wilderness shall waters break out, and streams in the desert" (Isaiah 55:13; 35:6).

Or perhaps you may say, "My life is all a tempest of sorrow or of temptation, and it will be a long while before I can walk beside any still waters." But your Shepherd said to the raging seas, "Peace, be still. And the wind ceased, and there was a great calm" (Mark 4:39). Can He not do it again?

Thousands of the flock of Christ can testify that when they put themselves completely into His hands, He has quieted the raging tempest and has turned their deserts into blossoming gardens. I do not mean that there will be no more outward trouble, care, or suffering; but, these very places will become green pastures and still waters inwardly to the soul.

The Shepherd knows what pastures are best for His sheep. They should not question or doubt, but must trustingly follow Him. Perhaps He sees that the best pastures for some of us are to be found in the midst of opposition or of earthly trials. If He leads you there, you may be sure they are green pastures for you where you will grow strong.

Words fail to tell half of what the good Shepherd does for the flock that trusts Him. According to His promise, He makes a covenant of peace with them and causes the evil beasts to cease out of the land. They will dwell safely in the wilderness and sleep in the woods. He makes them and the places around them a blessing. He causes the shower to come down in its season. These are showers of blessing. The tree of the field yields her fruit, and the earth yields her increase. They are safe in their land and are no more a prey to the heathen, and no one can make them afraid. (See Ezekiel 34:25-28.)

Surrendering To The Shepherd

You will probably ask how you can get the Lord to be your Shepherd. You do not need to get Him to be your Shepherd at all, for He already *is* your Shepherd. All that you must do is recognize that He is and yield yourself to His control.

When the announcement is made to children who have been longing for a little sister that one has just been born to them, they do not go on saying, "Oh, how we wish we had a little sister" or, "What can we do to get a little sister." But they begin at once to shout for joy and to dance about calling out to everybody, "Hurrah! Hurrah! We have a little sister now."

Likewise the announcement has been made to all of us by the angel of the Lord—"Fear not: for, behold, I bring you good tidings of great joy, which shall be to all people. For unto you is born this day in the city of David a Saviour, which is Christ the Lord" (Luke 2:10-11).

We have no need and no right to go on crying out, "Oh, if I only had a Savior" or, "What shall I do to make Christ my Savior?" He is already *born* our Savior. We need only to accept it for ourselves. Then we may rejoice that He is and give ourselves into His care.

There is nothing complicated about it. We are simply required to believe it and act as if it were true. Every soul that will begin today believing in the Good Shepherd and trusting itself to His care, will feed in His green pastures and walk beside His still waters.

What else can the Lord, who is our Shepherd, do with His sheep? He has no folds that are not good folds, no pastures that are not green pastures, and no waters but still waters. They may not look so outwardly; but we who have tried them can testify that His fold and His pastures are always places of peace and comfort to the inward life of the soul.

If you seem to have difficulty in understanding all this, and if the life of trust looks complicated and mysterious, I advise you not to try to understand it; simply begin to live it. Begin saying, "This is my Psalm, and I am going to believe it. I have always known it by heart, but it has never meant much to me. But now I have made up my mind to believe that the Lord is my Shepherd, and

70

that He will care for me as a shepherd cares for his sheep. I will not doubt nor question it again." Then abandon yourself to His care as the sheep abandon themselves to the care of their shepherd, trusting Him fully and following wherever He leads.

We must not forget that while sheep trust unconsciously and by instinct, we need to trust intelligently and deliberately. Our instincts, unfortunately are all against trusting. We have to make an effort to trust. We have to choose to do it.

But we can do this, however weak and ignorant we may be. We may not understand all it means to be a sheep of such a Shepherd, but He knows. If our faith will claim Him in this blessed and wondrous relationship, He will care for us according to His love and His wisdom and His power, and not according to our poor comprehension of it.

It seems as though we do not need any other passage from the whole Bible beside this nursery Psalm to make our lives full of comfort. There is no room left for the believer to worry, if he actually believes this Psalm. With the Lord for our Shepherd, how is it possible for anything to go wrong? With Him for our Shepherd, all that this Psalm promises must be ours.

When we have learned to know Him, we will be able to say with a triumph of trust, "Surely goodness and mercy shall follow me (pursue, overtake) all the days of my life: and I shall dwell in the house of the Lord forever" (Psalm 23:6). Even the future will lose all its terror for us, and our confidence in our Shepherd will deliver us from all fear of evil tidings.

In conclusion, you can enter into this relationship with Christ and be a helpless, docile, and trusting sheep. Believe that He is truly your Shepherd, caring for you with all the love, care, and tenderness that His name involves. Then follow Him wherever He leads, and you will soon lose all your old spiritual discomfort. "And the peace of God, which passeth all understanding, shall keep your hearts and minds through Christ Jesus" (Philippians 4:7).

Chapter 5

HE SPOKE OF THE FATHER

"They understood not that he spake to them of the Father"—John 8:27.

One of the most illuminating names of God is the one revealed by our Lord Jesus Christ—the name of *Father*. While God had been called throughout the ages by many other names expressing other aspects of His character, Christ alone revealed Him to us under the all-inclusive name of Father. It is a name that holds within itself all other names of wisdom and power, and, above all, of love and goodness. The name of Father embodies a perfect supply for all our needs.

Christ, who was the only begotten Son in the bosom of the Father, was the only one who could reveal this name, for He alone knew the Father. "As the Father knoweth me, even so know I the Father. . .Not that any man hath seen the Father, save he which is of God, he hath seen the Father" (John 10:15; 6:46).

In the Old Testament, God was not revealed as

the Father so much as a great warrior fighting for His people, or as a mighty King ruling over them and caring for them. The name of Father is only given to Him six or seven times at the most. In the New Testament, however, it is given between two and three hundred times.

Christ knew Him, and He was the only one who could reveal His Father. "No man knoweth. . .who the Father is, but the Son, and he to whom the Son will reveal him" (Luke 10:22).

The question that confronts each of us is whether we understand that Christ speaks to us of the Father. We know He uses the word *Father* continually, but do we understand what the word means? Have we even so much as an inkling of what the Father is?

A True Father

All the discomfort and unrest of the spiritual life of so many of God's children come from this: they do not understand that God is truly their Father. They think of Him as a stern Judge or a severe Taskmaster or, at best, as an unapproachable Dignitary, seated on a far-off throne, dispensing exacting laws for a frightened and trembling world. In terror that they might fail to meet His requirements, they hardly know which way to turn. But they have no conception of a God who is a Father, tender and loving and full of compassion; a God who, like a father, will be on their side against the whole universe.

Discomfort and unrest are impossible to the souls that come to know that God is their Father. God is the kind of Father that our highest instincts tell us a good father should be. Sometimes earthly fathers are unkind, tyrannical, selfish, or even cruel. Or they are merely indifferent and neglectful. None of these can be called good fathers. But God, who is good, must be a good Father or not a Father at all.

We must have all known good fathers in this world or at least can imagine them. I knew one, and he filled my childhood with sunshine. I can remember vividly with what confidence and triumph I walked through my days, absolutely secure in the knowledge that I had a wonderful father. I am very sure that I have learned a little about the perfect fatherhood of God, because of my experience with this lovely earthly father.

But God is not only a father; He is a mother as well. We have all known mothers whose love and tenderness have been without bound or limit. The God who created them both, and who is Himself father and mother in one, could never have created earthly fathers and mothers who were more tender and more loving than He is Himself. Therefore, if we want to know what sort of a Father He is, we must heap together all the best of all the fathers and mothers we have ever known or can imagine. Then we must tell ourselves that this is only a faint image of God, our Father in heaven.

When our Lord was teaching His disciples how

to pray, the only name by which He taught them to address God was "Our Father which art in heaven" (Matthew 6:9). This meant that we were to think of Him only in this light. Millions of times, during all the centuries since then, this name has been uttered by the children of God everywhere. Yet, how much has it been understood? Had all who used the name known what it meant, it would have been impossible for the misrepresentations of His character and the doubts of His love and care to have crept in that have so desolated the souls of His children throughout all the ages.

Tyranny, unkindness, and neglect might perhaps be attributed to a God whose name was only a king or a judge or a lawgiver. But of God who is before all else a father, and a good father, no such things could possibly be believed. Moreover, since He is an everlasting Father, He must act, always and under all circumstances, as a good father should act. It is inconceivable that a good father could forget, neglect, or be unfair to his children. A savage father or a wicked father might, but a good father—never!

When we call our God by the blessed name of Father, we know that, if He is a father at all, He must be the very best of fathers. It is a Fatherhood that combines both father and mother in one, in our highest ideals of both. It comprises all the love, tenderness, compassion, yearning, and all the self-sacrifice that we recognize to be the innermost soul of parentage, even though we may not always see it carried out by all earthly parents.

But what about the other names of God? Do they not convey other and more terrifying ideas? They only do so because this blessed name of Father is not added to them. This name must accompany every other name by which He has ever been known.

Has He been called a Judge? Yes, but He is a Father Judge, one who judges as a loving father would. Is He a King? Yes, but He is a King who is at the same time the Father of His subjects and rules them with a father's tenderness. Is He a Lawgiver? Yes, but He is a Lawgiver who gives laws as a father would, remembering the weakness and ignorance of his helpless children.

"Like as a father pitieth his children, so the Lord pitieth them that fear Him. For he knoweth our frame; he remembereth that we are dust" (Psalm 103:13-14). It is not "as a judge judges, so the Lord judges;" not "as a taskmaster controls, so the Lord controls;" not "as a lawgiver imposes laws, so the Lord imposes laws;" but, "as a father pitieth, so the Lord pitieth."

Never, never must we think of God in any other way than as our Father. All other attributes must be based upon and limited by this one of our Father. What a good father could not do, God, who is our Father, cannot do either. And what a good father should do, God, who is our Father, is absolutely sure to do.

A Measure Of His Love

In our Lord's prayer in John 17, He says that He has declared to us the name of the Father in order that we may discover the wonderful truth that the Father loves us *as* He loved His Son. Now, how many of us believe this? We have read this chapter over often. Yet, do any of us believe that it is an actual, tangible fact that God loves us as much as He loved Christ? If we believed this to be true, could we ever have an anxious or rebellious thought again?

We would be absolutely sure, under every conceivable circumstance, that the divine Father, who loves us just as much as He loved His only begotten Son, would care for us in the best possible way. We would be convinced that He could not deprive us of any good thing. No wonder our Lord could tell us so emphatically not to be anxious or troubled about anything; He knew His Father and knew that it was safe to trust Him completely.

It is very striking that He so often said, "your heavenly Father;" not Mine only, but yours. Your heavenly Father cares for the sparrows and the lilies. Of course He will care for you who are of so much more value than many sparrows. How supremely foolish it is for us to be worried and anxious about things, when Christ has said that our heavenly Father knows that we need all of these things. Being a good Father, He will supply our needs. (See Matthew 6:26-33.)

Our Lord draws the comparison between earthly fathers and our heavenly Father in order to show us how much more good and tender and willing our heavenly Father is to bless us. "If ye then, being evil, know how to give good gifts unto your children, how much more shall your Father which is in heaven give good things to them that ask him?" (Matthew 7:11).

Can we imagine a good earthly father giving a stone or a serpent to a hungry child, instead of bread or fish? Would not our soul despise a father who could do such things? Yet, there are a great many of God's children who think that their heavenly Father does this sort of thing to them. They believe He gives them stones when they ask for bread or curses when they ask for blessings.

It is not only that our heavenly Father is willing to give us good things. He is far more than willing. Our Lord says, "Fear not, little flock; for it is your Father's good pleasure to give you the kingdom" (Luke 12:32). There is no grudging in His giving; it is His good pleasure to give. He likes to do it. He wants to give you the Kingdom far more than you want to have it.

Those of us who are parents know how eager we are to give good things to our children—often far more eager than our children are to have them. This may help us to understand how it is that it is God's good pleasure to give us the Kingdom. Why then, should we ask Him in such fear and trembling? Why should we torment ourselves with the anxiety that He may fail to grant what we need? There can be only one answer to these questions: we do not know the Father.

We are told that we are "of the household of God" (Ephesians 2:19). The principle is set forth in the Bible that if any man does not provide for his own household, he has "denied the faith, and is worse than an infidel" (1 Timothy 5:8). Since we are of the household of God, this principle applies to Him. If He fails to provide for us, His own words would condemn Him. I say this reverently, but I want to say it emphatically, for so few people seem to realize it.

It was extremely significant to me to discover this responsibility of my Father in heaven. In a single moment, the burden of life was lifted from my shoulders and laid on His. All my fears, anxieties, and questionings dropped into the abyss of His loving care.

The instinct which demands that the parents who bring a child into the world are bound to care for and protect that child according to their best ability is a divinely implanted instinct. It is meant to teach the magnificent fact that the Creator, who has made human parents responsible for their children, is equally responsible toward His children.

I could have shouted for joy! From that glad hour, my troubles were over. For when this insight comes to a soul, that soul must enter into rest.

With such a God, who is also a Father, there is no room for anything but rest. When temptations to doubt or anxiety or fear come to me, I dare not listen to them. To do so would be to cast a doubt on the trustworthiness of my Father in heaven.

False Humility

We may have thought that our doubts and fears were because of our own unworthiness and arose from humility. We may even have taken them as a sign of special piety and thought they were in some way pleasing to God.

If children let in doubts of their parent's love and begin to fear their care may fail, would these doubts and fears be evidence of humility on the children's part? Would they be at all pleasing to their parents?

If God is our Father, the only thing we can do with doubts and fears and anxious thoughts is cast them all behind our backs and have nothing more to do with them ever again. We *can* do this. We can give up our doubts just as we would urge a drunkard to give up his drink. We can take a pledge against doubting, just as we try to induce the drunkard to take a pledge against drinking.

Once we see that our doubts are a sin against God and question His trustworthiness, we will be eager to give them up. We may have cherished our doubts because perhaps we thought they were a part of our religion. We may have thought they were a proper attitude of the soul in one so unworthy. But if we see that God is our Father, we will reject every doubt with horror, because it slanders our Father's love and care.

What more can any soul want than to have a God whose name is *our Father* and whose character and ways reach the highest possibilities of His name? As Philip said, "Lord, show us the Father and it sufficeth us" (John 14:8). It does indeed satisfy, beyond what words can express!

A Lesson In Trust

One day a friend of mine went to see a woman living in one of the poorest parts of Philadelphia. The woman's case had been reported as being one of great need. My friend found things even worse than she had feared. The poor woman was old and crippled with rheumatism. She lived alone in a little room, with only the help of a kind neighbor now and then to do things for her. Yet, she was bright and cheerful and full of thanksgiving for her many blessings.

My friend marveled that cheerfulness could be possible under such circumstances and said, "But do you ever get frightened at the thought of what may happen to you, all alone here, and so lame as you are?"

The old saint looked at her with surprise and said in a tone of amazement, "Frightened! Why, honey, doesn't you know I have got a Father, and doesn't you know He takes care of me the whole endurin' time?" And then, as my friend looked perplexed, she added in a tone of wondering reproof, "Why, honey, surely my Father is your Father, too, and you knows about Him, and you knows He always takes care of His chilluns." It was a lesson my friend never forgot.

"Behold, what manner of love the Father hath bestowed upon us, that we should be called the sons of God" (1 John 3:1). The manner of love bestowed upon us is the love of a father for his son. It is a tender, protecting love that knows our weakness and our need and cares for us accordingly. He treats us as sons. All He asks in return is that we treat Him as a Father, whom we can trust without anxiety.

We must take the son's place of dependence and trust and let Him keep the father's place of care and responsibility. Because we are the children and He is the Father, we must let Him do the father's part. Too often we take upon our own shoulders the father's part. We try to take care of and provide for ourselves. No good earthly father would want his children to take upon their young shoulders the burden of his duties. Much less would our heavenly Father want to lay the burden of His duties upon us.

No wonder we are told to cast all our care upon Him, for He cares for us. (See 1 Peter 5:7.) Of course He cares! It is His business as a Father to do so. He would not be a good Father if He did not. All He asks of us is to let Him know when we need anything. Then we should leave the supplying of that need to Him. He assures us that if we do this, the "peace of God which passeth all understanding shall keep your hearts and minds through Christ Jesus" (Philippians 4:7).

The children of a good human father are at peace because they trust in their father's care; but the children of the heavenly Father too often have no peace because they are afraid to trust in His care. They make their requests known to Him perhaps, but that is all they do. It is a sort of religious form they feel it is necessary to go through. But the idea that He will care for them seems to never cross their minds. Instead, they go on carrying their cares and burdens on their own shoulders, exactly as if they had no Father in heaven. It is as if they had never asked Him to care for them.

What utter folly it all is! For if ever an earthly father was worthy of the confidence of his children, much more is our heavenly Father worthy of our confidence. The reason that so few of His children trust Him can only be that they have not yet found out that He is their Father. Although they may call Him Father every day in their prayers, they still have never seen that He is the sort of Father that a good and true human father is: a Father who is loving, tender, and merciful. They fail to realize that He is full of kindness toward the helpless beings whom He has brought into existence and whom He is therefore bound to protect.

The Spirit of Adoption

The remedy for your discomfort and unrest is to be found in becoming acquainted with the Father. "For ye have not received the spirit of bondage again to fear; but ye have received the Spirit of adoption, whereby we cry, Abba, Father" (Romans 8:15).

Is it this Spirit of adoption that reigns in your hearts or is it the spirit of bondage? Your whole comfort in your spiritual life depends upon which spirit it is. No amount of wrestling or agonizing, no prayers and no efforts, will be able to bring you comfort while the Spirit of adoption is lacking in your heart.

You may ask how you are to get this Spirit of adoption. I can only say that it is not a thing to be acquired. It comes as the result of the discovery that God is truly a Father.

When you have made this discovery you cannot help feeling like a child and acting like a child. This is what the Spirit of adoption means. It is nothing mysterious. Rather, it is the simple, natural result of having found a Father where you thought there was only a Judge.

Every soul has great need to make this supreme discovery. And to do this, we have only to see what Christ tells us about the Father, and then believe it. "Verily, verily, I say unto thee, We speak that we do know, and testify that we have seen." Then

He adds sadly, "Ye receive not our witness" (John 3:11.)

In order to come to the knowledge of the Father, we must receive the testimony of Christ who declares, "The words that I speak unto you I speak not of myself: but the Father that dwelleth in me, he doeth the works" (John 14:10). After grieving over the fact that so few received His testimony, He adds these memorable words, "He that hath received his testimony hath set to his seal that God is true" (John 3:33).

The whole authority of Christ stands or falls with this. If we receive His testimony, we set to our seal that God is true. If we reject that testimony, we make Him a liar.

"If ye had known me," says Christ, "ye should have known my Father also: and from henceforth ye know him, and have seen him" (John 14:7). The thing for us to do then is to make up our minds that from now on we will receive His testimony, and will know the Father. Let other people worship whatever sort of a God they may; for us there must be "but one God even the Father."

"For though there be that are called gods, whether in heaven or in earth, (as there be gods many, and lords many,) But to us there is but one God, the Father, of whom are all things, and we in him; and one Lord Jesus Christ, by whom are all things, and we by him" (1 Corinthians 8:5).

Chapter 6

GOD'S CHARACTER REVEALED

"That men may know that thou, whose name alone is JEHOVAH, art the most high over all the earth"—Psalm 83:18.

Among all the names of God, perhaps the most comprehensive is the name Jehovah. Cruden describes this name as the unutterable name of God. The word Jehovah means the Self-Existing One, the "I AM." It is generally used as a direct revelation of who God is. In several places an explanatory word is added, revealing one of His special characteristics. It is to these that I particularly want to call attention. They are as follows:

Jehovah-jireh—The Lord will see, or the Lord will provide.

Jehovah-nissi—The Lord our Banner.

Jehovah-shalom—The Lord our Peace.

Jehovah-tsidkenu—The Lord our Righteousness.

Jehovah-shammah—The Lord is there.

These names were discovered by God's people in times of need; that is, the characteristics the names describe were discovered. The names were the natural expression of these characteristics.

The Lord Will Provide

When Abraham was about to sacrifice his son and saw no way of escape, the Lord provided a lamb for the sacrifice and delivered Isaac. Abraham made the grand discovery that it was one of the characteristics of Jehovah to see and provide for the needs of His people. Therefore, he called Him Jehovah-jireh—the Lord will see, or the Lord will provide.

The parallels to this in the New Testament are numerous. Our Lord urges us to not worry about anything, because God cares for us. "Your heavenly Father knoweth that ye have need of all these things" (Matthew 6:32).

If the Lord sees and knows our need, it will be only natural for Him to provide for it. Being our Father, He could not do anything else. As soon as a good mother sees that her child needs anything, she immediately sets about supplying that need. She does not even wait for the child to ask. The sight of the need is a request in itself. Being a good mother, she could not do otherwise.

When God says to us, "I see your need," He in reality says also, "I am your Provider." He cannot see and fail to provide.

"Why do I not have everything I want then?" you may ask. Only because God sees that what you want is not really the thing you need, but probably exactly the opposite. In order to give us what we need, the Lord is often obliged to keep from us what we want.

Your heavenly Father knows what things you need. You do not know. If all your wants were gratified, it might be that all your needs would be left unsupplied. It should satisfy us that God is indeed Jehovah-jireh—the Lord who will see and provide.

A great many Christians today have never made Abraham's discovery. They do not know that the Lord is Jehovah-jireh. They are trusting Him to save their souls in the future, but they never dream He wants to carry their cares for them now.

They are like a man with a heavy load on his back who was given a lift by a friend. He thankfully climbed into the vehicle, but still kept his burden on his back, bowed down under the weight of it.

"Why do you not put your burden down on the bottom of the carriage?" asked his friend.

"Oh," replied the man, "it is a great deal to ask you to carry me, and I could not ask you to carry my burden also."

You wonder how anyone could be so silly, and yet are you not doing the same? Are you trusting the Lord to take care of you, but still carrying your burdens on your own shoulders? Who is the silliest—that man or you?

The Banner Of The Lord

Jehovah-nissi "The Lord my Banner." This discovery was made by Moses when Amalek came to fight with Israel in Rephidim. The Lord gave the Israelites a glorious victory. Moses realized that the Lord was fighting for them, and he built an altar to Jehovah-nissi, "The Lord my Banner."

The Bible is full of this name. "The Lord is a man of war" (Exodus 15:3); "The Lord your God, he it is that fighteth for you" (Joshua 24:10); "The Lord shall fight for you, and ye shall hold your peace" (Exodus 14:14); "Be not afraid nor dismayed by reason of this great multitude; for the battle is not yours, but God's" (2 Chronicles 20:15); "God Himself is with us for our captain" (2 Chronicles 13:12).

Nothing is more abundantly expressed in the Bible than this: the Lord will fight for us, if we will let Him. He knows that we have no strength or might against our spiritual enemies. Like a tender mother when her helpless children are attacked by an enemy, He fights for us. All He asks of us is to be still and let Him do it. This is the only sort of spiritual conflict that is ever successful.

We are very slow to learn this however. When temptations come, instead of handing the battle over to the Lord, we summon all our forces to fight them ourselves. We believe that the Lord is somewhere near, and if the worst comes, He will step in to help us; but for the most part, we feel that we must do all the fighting.

Our method of fighting consists of a series of repentings and making resolutions and promises. We go through some weary struggles for victory. Then failing again, we start over with repentance and resolutions and promises and renewed struggles. Each time we tell ourselves that now at last we certainly will have the victory. And each time we fail even worse than before. This may go on for weeks, months, or even years, and no real or permanent deliverance ever comes.

The Good Fight

You may ask, "Are we not to do any fighting ourselves?" Of course we are to fight, but not in this fashion. We are to fight the good fight of faith, as Paul exhorted Timothy. (See 1 Timothy 6:12.)

The fight of faith is not a fight of effort or of struggle, but it is a fight of trusting. It is the kind of fight that Hezekiah fought when he and his army marched out to meet their enemy. They sang songs of victory as they went, and they found that their enemy was dead. Our part in this fight is to hand the battle over to the Lord and to trust Him for the victory.

We are to put on His armor, not our own. Paul tells us what it is in Ephesians 6:14-17. It is the girdle of truth, the breastplate of righteousness, and the shoes of the preparation of the gospel of peace. It is the helmet of salvation and the sword

91

of the Spirit, which is the Word of God. Above all, he says we are to take the shield of faith with which we shall be able to quench all the fiery darts of the wicked. There is nothing here about promises or resolutions; nothing about hours and days of agonizing struggles and bitter remorse.

"Above all things taking the shield of faith." Faith is the one essential thing; without it, all else is useless. It means that we must not only hand the battle over to the Lord, but we must leave it with Him in absolute faith that He will conquer.

It is here where the fight comes in. It seems so unsafe to sit still and do nothing but trust the Lord. The temptation to take the battle back into our own hands is often tremendous.

To keep hands off in spiritual matters is as hard for us as it is for the drowning man to keep hands off the one who is trying to rescue him. We all know how impossible it is to rescue a drowning man who tries to help his rescuer. It is equally impossible for the Lord to fight our battles for us when we insist upon trying to fight them ourselves. It is not that He will not, but He cannot. Our interference hinders His working. Spiritual forces cannot work while earthly forces are active.

Our Lord tells us that without Him we can do nothing. We have read and repeated His words hundreds of times, but does anyone believe they are actually true?

If we were to drag out into the light our secret thoughts on the subject, would we find them to be something like this: "When Christ said those words, He meant to say that we cannot of ourselves do much, or at any rate no great things. But nothing? No, that is impossible. We are not babies, and we are certainly meant to use all the strength we have in fighting our enemies. When our own strength gives out, we can then call upon the Lord to help us."

In spite of all our failures, we cannot help thinking that, if only we would try harder and be more persistent, we would be equal to any encounter. But we overlook the fact that our natural powers are of no use in spiritual regions or with spiritual enemies.

Just as our skill in walking on the earth would not help us if we had to fly in the air, so our natural powers are of no use in spiritual warfare. If we try to depend on them, they are a real hindrance, just as trying to walk would hinder us if we sought to float or to fly.

Spiritual Wrestling And Unbelief

We can easily see, therefore, that the result of trusting in ourselves when dealing with our spiritual enemies will inevitably be very serious. It not only causes failure, but in the end it causes rebellion. A great deal of what is called spiritual conflict might better be named spiritual rebellion.

God told us to cease from our own efforts and to hand our battles over to Him. Then we bluntly refuse to obey Him. True, we do fight; however, it is not a fight of faith, but a fight of unbelief.

Our spiritual wrestling, of which we are often so proud, is really a wrestling not for God, but against Him. We allow ourselves to indulge in doubts and fears; consequently, we are plunged into darkness, turmoil, and wrestlings of spirit. We call this spiritual conflict and look upon ourselves as an interesting and peculiar case. The word that explains our peculiar case is the word *unbelief*. The simple remedy is to be found in the word *faith*.

"But," you may ask, "what about wrestling Jacob?" (See Genesis 32:24-25.) "Did he not gain his victory by wrestling?" On the contrary, he gained his victory by being made so weak that he could not wrestle any longer. It was not Jacob who wrestled with the angel, but the angel who wrestled with Jacob. Jacob was the one to be overcome. When the angel found that Jacob's resistance was so great that he could not prevail against him, the angel was obliged to lame him, by putting his thigh out of joint; and then the victory was won.

As soon as Jacob was too weak to resist any longer, he prevailed with God. He gained power when he lost it. He conquered when he could no longer fight.

Jacob's experience is like ours. The Lord wrestles with us in order to bring us to a place of entire dependence on Himself. We resist as long as we have any strength. At last He is forced to bring us to a place of helplessness, where we are obliged to yield. Then we conquer by this very yielding.

Our victory is always the victory of weakness. Paul knew this victory when he said, "And he said unto me, My grace is sufficient for thee: for my strength is made perfect in weakness. Most gladly therefore will I rather glory in my infirmities, that the power of Christ may rest upon me. Therefore I take pleasure in infirmities, in reproaches, in necessities, in persecutions, in distresses for Christ's sake: for when I am weak, then am I strong" (2 Corinthians 12:9-10). Who would ask for a more magnificent victory than this! This victory will be ours, if we take the Lord to be our Banner and commit all our battles to Him.

The Lord Our Peace

The name of Jehovah-shalom, or "The Lord our Peace," was discovered by Gideon. The Lord had called him to a work that he felt utterly unfit to attempt.

"Oh, my Lord," he had said, "wherewith shall I save Israel? behold, my family is poor in Manasseh, and I am the least of my father's house. And the Lord said unto him, Surely I will be with thee, and thou shalt smite the Midianites as one man. . . .And the Lord said unto him, Peace be unto thee; fear not: thou shalt not die" (Judges 6:15-16, 23).

Then Gideon believed the Lord. Although the battle had not yet been fought and no victories had been won, with the eye of faith, he saw peace already secured. He built an altar to the Lord and called it Jehovah-shalom, which means "The Lord our Peace."

Of all the needs of the human heart, none is greater than the need of peace; and none is more abundantly promised in the gospel. "Peace I leave with you," says our Lord, "my peace I give unto you. . . .Let not your heart be troubled, neither let it be afraid" (John 14:27). And again He says, "These things have I spoken unto you, that in me ye might have peace. In the world ye shall have tribulation: but be of good cheer; I have overcome the world" (John 16:33).

Our idea of peace is that it must be outward before it can be inward. That is, all enemies must be driven away, and then all troubles will cease. But the Lord's idea was of an interior peace that could exist in the midst of turmoil and could be triumphant over it. The foundation of this sort of peace is found in the fact, not that we have overcome the world or that we ever can, but that Christ has overcome it.

Only the conqueror can proclaim peace. The people whose battles he has fought can do nothing but enter into it. They can neither make nor unmake it. But if they choose, they can refuse to believe in it and fail to let it reign in their hearts.

You may be afraid to believe that Christ has made peace for you; so you live on in a weary state of warfare. Nevertheless, He has done it, and all your continued warfare is worse than useless.

The Bible tells us that Christ is our peace; therefore, whether I feel as if I have peace or not, peace is mine in Christ. I must take possession of it by faith. Faith is simply to believe and assert the thing that God says.

If He says there is peace, faith agrees and enters into the enjoyment of it. If He has proclaimed peace in the Bible, I must proclaim it in my own heart, whatever the circumstances are. "The kingdom of God is. . .righteousness, and peace, and joy, in the Holy Ghost" (Romans 14:17). The soul that has not taken possession of peace has not yet fully entered into this Kingdom.

We can always enter into peace by a simple obedience to Philippians 4:6-7. "Be careful for nothing; but in every thing by prayer and supplication with thanksgiving let your requests be made known unto God. And the peace of God, which passeth all understanding, shall keep your hearts and minds through Christ Jesus."

The steps here are very plain, and they are only two. First, give up all anxiety, and second, hand over your cares to God. Then stand steadfastly here, and peace must come. It simply must, for there is no room for anything else.

The Lord Our Righteousness

The name Jehovah-tsidkenu, "The Lord our Righteousness," was revealed by the Lord through the prophet Jeremiah when he was announcing the coming of Christ. "Behold, the days come, saith the Lord, that I will raise unto David a righteous Branch, and a King shall reign and prosper, and shall execute judgment and justice in the earth. In his days Judah shall be saved, and Israel shall dwell safely: and this is his name whereby he shall be called, THE LORD OUR RIGHTEOUSNESS" (Jeremiah 23:5-6).

Most of the struggles and conflicts of our Christian life come from our fights with sin and our efforts to pursue righteousness. How great are our failures! As long as we try to conquer sin or obtain righteousness by our own efforts, we are bound to fail. But if we discover that the Lord is our righteousness, we have gotten hold of the secret of victory.

In the Lord Jesus Christ we have a fuller revelation of this wonderful name of God. The apostle Paul, the ambassador for Christ, declares that God made Christ "to be sin for us who knew no sin; that we might be made the righteousness of God in him" (2 Corinthians 5:21). "But of him are ye in Christ Jesus who of God is made unto us wisdom, and righteousness, and sanctification, and redemption" (1 Corinthians 1:30).

Very few Christians understand what this means. We repeat the words as belonging to our religious vocabulary; and in a vague sort of way, we think of them as being somehow a part of the salvation of

Christ. But we have very little concrete idea of their practical use.

This name of God, the Lord our Righteousness, has tremendously practical use. We are not to try to have a stock of righteousness laid up in ourselves from which to draw a supply when needed. Rather, we are to draw continual fresh supplies from the righteousness that is laid up for us in Christ. If we need righteousness of any sort, such as patience, humility, or love, it is useless for us to look within, hoping to find a supply there. We never will find it. We must simply take it by faith, as a possession that is stored up for us in Christ, who is our righteousness.

The results are triumphant. I have seen sweetness and gentleness poured like a flood of sunshine into dark and bitter spirits. It happened when the hand of faith reached out to grasp them as a present possession, stored up for all who are in Christ. I have seen sharp tongues made tender, anxious hearts made calm, and fretful spirits made quiet by faith in the righteousness that is ours in Christ.

Paul, after proving to us in the third chapter of Romans the absolute impossibility of obtaining righteousness through the law (that is, by our own efforts) goes on to say, ''But now the righteousness of God without the law is manifested, being witnessed by the law and the prophets; Even the righteousness of God which is by faith of Jesus Christ unto all and upon all them that believe: for there is no difference" (Romans 3:21-22).

It is faith and faith only that can appropriate this righteousness that is ours in Christ. We appropriate by faith the forgiveness that is ours in Christ. So we must also appropriate by faith the patience that is ours in Him or the gentleness, meekness, long-suffering, or any other virtue we may need. Our own efforts will not achieve righteousness for us, any more than they will obtain forgiveness.

And yet how many Christians try! Paul describes them when he says, "For I bear them record that they have a zeal of God, but not according to knowledge. For they being ignorant of God's righteousness, and going about to establish their own righteousness, have not submitted themselves unto the righteousness of God. For Christ is the end of the law for righteousness to every one that believeth" (Romans 10:2-4).

I pray that all such zealous souls discover this wonderful name of God, the Lord our Righteousness! If only they would give up seeking to establish their own righteousness, and would submit themselves to the righteousness of God. Isaiah tells us, "All our righteousness are as filthy rags" (Isaiah 64:6). Paul prays that he may be found in Christ, "not having mine own righteousness, which is of the law, but that which is through the faith of Christ, the righteousness which is of God by faith" (Philippians 3:9).

Do we comprehend the meaning of this prayer?

Are we prepared to join in it with our whole hearts? If so, our struggle after righteousness will be over. Jehovah-tsidkenu will supply all our needs.

The Lord Is There

The name Jehovah-shammah, or "The Lord is There," was revealed to the prophet Ezekiel. He was shown by a vision what was to be the future home of the children of Israel. He described the land and the city of Jerusalem and ended his description by saying, "And the name of the city from that day shall be, The Lord is there" (Ezekiel 48:35).

This name includes all the others. Wherever the Lord is, everything must go well for His children. Where the good mother is, all goes well, according to her ability, for her children. How much more God cares for us. His presence is enough.

All through the Old Testament, the Lord's universal answer to all the fears and anxieties of the children of Israel was the simple words, "I will be with thee." He did not need to say anything more. His presence was to them a perfect guarantee that all their needs would be supplied; and the moment they were assured of it, they were no longer afraid to face the fiercest foe.

You may say, "If the Lord would only say the same thing to me, I would not be afraid either." Well, He has said it in unmistakable terms. When the angel of the Lord announced to Joseph the coming birth of Christ, he said, "They shall call his name Emmanuel, which being interpreted is, God with us" (Matthew 2:23). This short sentence reveals to us the grandest fact the world can ever know—that God, the Almighty God, the Creator of heaven and earth, is not a far-off God, dwelling in a heaven of unapproachable glory. He has come down in Christ to dwell with us right here in this world, in the midst of our poor, ignorant, helpless lives. He is as close to us as we are to ourselves. If we believe in Christ at all, we must believe His name is "God with us." Both of these names, Jehovah-shammah and Emmanuel, mean the same thing. They mean that God is present everywhere in His universe, surrounding and sustaining everything, and holding all of us in His safe and blessed care. They mean that we can find no place in all His universe of which it cannot be said, "The Lord is there."

The psalmist says, "Whither shall I go from thy spirit? or whither shall I flee from thy presence? If I ascend up into heaven thou art there: if I make my bed in hell, behold, thou art there. If I take the wings of the morning, and dwell in the uttermost parts of the sea; Even there shall thy hand lead me, and thy right hand shall hold me" (Psalm 139:7-10).

We cannot drift from the love and care of an ever-present God. Christians who think He has forsaken them and who cry out for His presence are crying out in ignorance of the fact that He is always and everywhere present with them. In truth, they cannot get out of His presence, even if they try. Oh, if only they knew this wonderful and satisfying name of God!

"Speak to Him, thou, for He hears; and spirit with spirit may meet; Closer is He than breathing, and nearer than hands and feet."

Abundance Of Grace

Let us sum up the teaching of these five names of God. What is it they say to us?

Jehovah-jireh—"I am He who sees your need, and therefore I provide for it."

Jehovah-nissi—"I am your Captain and your Banner, and I am He who will fight your battles for you."

Jehovah-shalom—"I am your peace. I have made peace for you, and My peace I give to you."

Jehovah-tsidkenu—"I am your righteousness. In Me you will find all you need of wisdom, righteousness, sanctification, and redemption."

Jehovah-shammah—"I am with you. I am your ever-present, all-encompassing God and Savior. I will never leave you or forsake you. Wherever you go, there I am, and My hand will hold you."

All this is true, whether we know it and recognize it or not. We may have gone through our lives starved, weary, and wretched. But all the time we have been starving in the midst of plenty. The fullness of God's salvation has awaited our faith and an abundance of grace and the gift of righteousness have awaited our receiving.

I pray that Christians would see that these all-embracing names of God leave no corner of their need unsupplied. Then would they be able to testify with the prophet Isaiah to all around them, "Behold, God is my salvation; I will trust, and not be afraid: for the Lord Jehovah is my strength and my song; he also is become my salvation. Therefore with joy shall we draw water out of the wells of salvation" (Isaiah 12:2-3).

Chapter 7

THE LORD IS GOOD

"O taste and see that the Lord is good: blessed is the man that trusteth in him"—Psalm 34:8.

Have you ever asked yourself what you honestly think of God? Do you believe Him to be a good God or a bad God? Perhaps this question shocks you. You may be horrified at the suggestion that you could possibly think that God is a bad God. But before you have finished this chapter, some of you will acknowledge that unconsciously perhaps, but nonetheless truly, you have by your doubts and complaints attributed to Him a character that you would not want to have attributed to yourself.

I will never forget the hour when I first discovered that God was good. I had of course always known that the Bible said He was good, but I thought it only meant He was religiously good. It never dawned on me that it meant He was actually and practically good, with the same kind of goodness He commanded us to have. The expression "the goodness of God" seemed to me nothing more than a sort of heavenly statement, which I could not be expected to understand.

Then one day while reading the Bible, I came across the words, "O taste and see that the Lord is good." Suddenly, they meant something. The Lord is good, I repeated to myself. What does it mean to be good? To be good is exactly the opposite of being bad. To be bad is to know the right and not do it, but to be good is to do the best we know. Since God is omniscient, He must know what is the best and highest good of all; therefore His goodness must necessarily be beyond question.

I can never express what this meant to me. I had a view of the goodness of God that I felt nothing could possibly go wrong under His care. It seemed to me that no one could ever be anxious again. Ever since that time, when I have been tempted to question whether He had been unkind, neglectful, or indifferent, I have been brought up short by the words, "The Lord is good." It is unthinkable that a God who is good could have done the bad things I imagined.

Your Image Of God

You may cringe at the suggestion that you could, under any circumstances, attribute something bad to God. Yet, you do not hesitate to accuse Him of doing things which you would consider to be most dishonorable and unkind if a friend did the same things.

For instance, Christians get into trouble; all

looks dark, and they have no sense of the Lord's presence. They begin to wonder whether the Lord has forsaken them. Sometimes they even accuse Him of indifference and neglect. They never realize that these accusations are tantamount to saying that the Lord does not keep His promises. They are declaring that He does not treat them as kindly and honorably as they expect their human friends to treat them. If one of our human friends left us because we were in trouble, we would not consider him to be a very good friend. How is it that we can, even for one moment, accuse our Lord of such actions?

If the Lord is good, not omnipotent only, but *good,* it must be because He always, under every circumstance, acts up to the highest ideal of goodness. Goodness in Him must mean, just as it does with us, the living up to the best and highest He knows.

Practically then, it means that He will not neglect any of His duties toward us. He will always treat us in the best possible way. This may sound like a platitude, and you may exclaim, "Why tell us this, for it is what we all believe?" But do you? If you did, would it be possible for you ever to think He was neglectful or indifferent or unkind or self-absorbed or inconsiderate?

Do not put on a righteous attitude and say, "Oh, but I never do accuse Him of any such things. I would not dare to." Don't you? Have you ever blamed Him for things you would scorn to do yourself?

How was it when that last grievous disappointment came your way? Did you feel as if the Lord had been unkind in permitting such a thing to come upon you when you were trying so hard to serve Him? Do you ever look upon His will as a tyrannical and arbitrary will that must be submitted to, but that could not possibly be loved? Does it ever seem to you a hard thing to say, "Thy will be done"? Would it seem so hard if you really believed that the Lord is good, and that He always does that which is good?

It is important to drag out our secret thoughts and feelings about the Lord into the full light of the Holy Spirit. Then we may see what our attitude about Him truly is. It is fatally easy to get into a habit of thinking wrong thoughts about God. Such thoughts will separate us from Him by a wide gulf of doubt and unbelief. More than anything else, more even than sin, wrong thoughts about God weaken the foundations of our spiritual life and grieve His heart of love.

We can understand this from our own experience. Nothing grieves us so much as to have our friends misjudge and misunderstand us and attribute to us motives we scorn. And nothing so grieves the Lord. It is in fact idolatry. For what is idolatry but creating and worshipping a false god. We are doing this very thing when we allow ourselves to misjudge Him and attribute to Him actions and feelings that are unkind and untrustworthy.

In the Bible it is called speaking against God. "Yea, they spake against God; they said, Can God furnish a table in the wilderness?" (Psalm 78:19). This seemed a very innocent question to ask. But God promised to supply all their needs in the wilderness. To ask this question implied a lack of confidence in His ability to do as He promised; it was therefore, in spite of its innocent appearance, a "speaking against" Him. A good God could not have led His people into the wilderness, and then have failed to provide for them. To question whether He was able to do it was to imply that He was not good.

We are sometimes sorely tempted to ask a similar question. Circumstances often make it seem impossible for God to supply our needs, and we find ourselves tempted to speak against Him by asking if He is able. Though He has blessed us many times before, we seem unable to believe He can do it again. In our hearts we limit Him because we do not believe His Word or trust in His goodness.

If our faith was what it should be, no circumstances could make us limit the power of God to supply our needs. The God who can make circumstances can surely control circumstances. Even in the wilderness, He can furnish a table for all who trust in Him.

There are many questions to be found in the Bible which cast doubts upon the goodness of God. Each one is a duplicate of questions asked by God's children today.

Let us consider a few of these questions and see whether we can find any counterparts to them in our own hearts.

"Is the Lord among us, or not?" (Exodus 17:7). God has declared to us in unmistakable terms, as He did to the children of Israel, that He is always with us. He will never leave or forsake us. Yet when trouble comes, we begin, as they did, to doubt His Word and question whether He really can be there. When the Israelites did this, Moses called it "tempting the Lord." (See Exodus 17:7.) It deserves the same condemnation when we do it.

No one can ask such a question without casting a doubt upon the truthfulness and trustworthiness of the Lord. To even ask it is to insult Him and to slander His character. It is, unfortunately, a common question even among God's own children. Many of them think it is only true humility to ask it. Such unworthy creatures, as they feel themselves to be, would be at the height of presumption to be confident of His presence with them.

But what about His own Word in the matter? He declared to us that He is with us, and He will never leave us or forsake us. Dare we make Him a liar by questioning the truth of His Word? A good

God cannot lie. We must give up forever asking such a question as this. The Lord is with us as truly as we are with ourselves. We simply have to believe that He is, no matter what the appearances may be.

"Is his mercy clean gone for ever? doth his promise fail for evermore?" (Psalm 77:8). To ask these two questions of a good God is to insult Him. It would be just as impossible for His mercy to leave us forever, as it would be for the tender mercies of a mother to come to an end. The psalmist said, "The Lord is good to all: and his tender mercies are over all his works" (Psalm 145:9). No matter how circumstances may look, we may be sure of this: God is good, and no promise of His has ever failed or can ever fail. Heaven and earth may pass away, but His Word will never pass away. (See Mark 13:31.)

"Hath God forgotten to be gracious?" (Psalm 77:9). To ask this question is to speak of Him as grievously as it would be to ask a good mother if she had forgotten her child. The Lord Himself says, "Can a woman forget her sucking child?. . .yea, they may forget, yet will I not forget thee" (Isaiah 49:15). A mother knows how grieved and insulted she would feel if anyone suggested the possibility of her forgetting her children. A mother at least should be able to understand how such questioning must grieve the Lord.

"Why hast thou made me thus?" (Romans 9:20). There is hardly one of us who has not been

111

tempted to speak against God in reference to our own personal make-up. We do not like our peculiar temperaments or characteristics. We long to be like someone else who has, we think, greater gifts of appearance or talent. We are discontented with our make-up, both inward and outward. We feel sure that all our failures are because of our unfortunate temperaments. Then we blame our Creator for having made us this way.

Learning Self-Acceptance

I remember a time in my life when I was tempted to be very rebellious about my own personality. I was a plain-spoken, energetic sort of an individual, trying to be a good Christian, but with no special air of spirituality about me. I had a sister who was so saintly in her looks and so reverent in her manner, that she seemed to be the embodiment of a true Christian.

I was sure I could be a better Christian if only I could get her saintly looks and manner. But all my struggles were useless. My natural temperament was far too energetic and outspoken for any appearance of saintliness. Many times I said reproachfully in my heart to God, "Why hast Thou made me thus?"

Then one day I came across a sentence in an old book that opened my eyes. It was as follows: "Be content to be what thy God has made thee." It flashed on me that God had made me and that He must know the sort of creature He wanted me to be. If He had made me a potato vine, I must be satisfied and grow potatoes and must not want to be a rose bush to grow roses. If He had fashioned me for humble tasks, I must be content to let others do the grander work. "For we are his workmanship, created in Christ Jesus unto good works, which God hath before ordained that we should walk in them" (Ephesians 2:10). God is good; therefore, His workmanship must be good also. We may securely trust that He will make out of us something that will be to His glory, no matter how unlikely this may seem to us.

The psalmist seemed to delight in repeating this blessed refrain, "For the Lord is good." He exhorted everybody to join him in saying it. "Let the redeemed of the Lord say so" was his earnest cry. (Psalm 107:2).

We must join our voices with his—"The Lord is good!" But we must not say it with our lips only, and then by our actions deny our words. We must say it with our whole being, with thought, word, and action. Then people will see we mean it and will be convinced that it is a tremendous truth.

A great many things in God's divine providence do not look like goodness to the physical eye. In reading the Psalms, we wonder how the psalmist could say, after some of the things he records, "For his mercy endureth forever" (Psalm 136:1). But faith sits down in the face of mysteries such as these and says, "The Lord is good; therefore all that He does must be good, no matter how it looks. I can wait for His explanations."

God's Housekeeping

A housekeeping illustration has often helped me here. I have a friend whom I know to be a good housekeeper. I do not become disturbed when at house-cleaning time things in her house are out of order. Carpets are rolled up and furniture shrouded in coverings. Painting and decorating make some rooms temporarily uninhabitable.

I say to myself, "My friend is a good housekeeper. Although things look so uncomfortable now, all this mess is here only because she plans to make it far more comfortable than it ever was before."

Similarly, this world is God's housekeeping. Although things look grievously upset, we know that He is good, and therefore must be a good Housekeeper. We may be perfectly sure that all this present upset will finally bring about a far better state of things. We have all felt at times as though we could have done God's housekeeping better than He does it Himself; but when we realize that God is good, we can feel this way no longer.

It comforts me enormously that, when the world seems to be going all wrong, I can just say to myself, "It is not my housekeeping, but it is the

Lord's. The Lord is good; therefore, His house-keeping must be good, too. It is foolish for me to be troubled."

A Christian who had learned to let God do the housekeeping was asked by a despairing child of God, "Does the world look like a wreck to you?"

"Yes," was the reply, in a tone of cheerful confidence. "Yes, like the wreck of a bursting seed."

Any of us who have watched the first sproutings of an oak tree from the heart of a decaying acorn will understand what this means. Before the acorn can bring forth the oak, it must be broken. No plant ever came from anything but a wrecked seed.

Our Lord uses this illustration to teach us the meaning of His dealings with us. "Verily, verily, I say unto you, Except a corn of wheat fall into the ground and die, it abideth alone: but if it die, it bringeth forth much fruit" (John 12:24).

The whole explanation of the apparent wreckage of the world or of our personal lives is set forth here. We can understand how our good God can permit the existence of sorrow and wrong in the world He has created and in the lives of the human beings He loves. It is His goodness that compels Him to permit it. For He knows that only through such apparent wreckage can the fruition of His glorious purpose for us come to pass. And we whose hearts also long for that fruition will, if we understand His ways, be able to praise Him for all His goodness, even when things seem hardest and most mysterious.

Paul tells us that the will of God is good and acceptable and perfect. (See Romans 12:2.) The will of a good God cannot help being good—in fact, it must be perfect. When we come to know this, we always find it acceptable; that is, we come to love it.

I am convinced that all trouble about submitting to the will of God would disappear if we could see clearly that His will is good. We struggle in vain to submit to a will that we do not believe to be good; but when we see that it is genuinely good, we submit to it with delight. We want it to be accomplished. Our hearts spring out to meet it.

Time fails me to tell all of the infinite goodness of the Lord. Each person must taste and see for themselves. If you will do it honestly and faithfully, the words of the psalmist will become true of you: "They shall abundantly utter the memory of thy great goodness, and shall sing of thy righteousness" (Psalm 145:7).

Chapter 8

THE LORD OUR DWELLING PLACE

"Lord, thou hast been our dwelling place in all generations"—Psalm 90:1.

The comfort or discomfort of our outward lives depends more upon the dwelling place of our bodies than upon almost any other material thing. Likewise, the comfort or discomfort of our inward life depends upon the dwelling place of our souls.

Our dwelling place is the place where we live and not the place we merely visit. It is our home. All the interests of our earthly lives are bound up in our homes. We do all we can to make them attractive and comfortable.

But our souls need a comfortable dwelling place even more than our bodies. Inward comfort is of far greater importance than outward comfort. Where the soul is full of peace and joy, outward surroundings are of comparatively little importance.

It is vital that we find out where our souls are living. The Lord declares that He has been our dwelling place in all generations. Now the question is, "Are we living in our dwelling place?"

The psalmist says of the children of Israel, "They wandered in the wilderness in a solitary way; they found no city to dwell in. Hungry and thirsty, their soul fainted in them" (Psalm 107:4-5).

There are many wandering souls in the Church whom this description of the Israelites would fit exactly. All their Christian lives they have been wandering in a spiritual wilderness and have found no city to dwell in. Hungry and thirsty, their souls have fainted in them. All the while, the door to the dwelling place of God has been standing wide open. The Father Himself invites them to come in and live there forever.

Our Lord urges this invitation upon us. "Abide in me, and I in you. As the branch cannot bear fruit of itself, except it abide in the vine; no more can ye, except ye abide in me. I am the vine, ye are the branches; He that abideth in me, and I in him, the same bringeth forth much fruit: for without me ye can do nothing. If a man abide not in me, he is cast forth as a branch, and is withered; and men gather them, and cast them into the fire, and they are burned. If ye abide in me, and my words abide in you, ye shall ask what ye will, and it shall be done unto you" (John 15:4-7).

Our souls are made for God. He is our natural home, and we can never be at rest anywhere else. "My soul longeth, yea, even fainteth for the courts of the Lord: my heart and my flesh crieth out for the living God" (Psalm 84:2). We always hunger and faint for the courts of the Lord, as long as we fail to make our home there.

A Rock And A Refuge

How can we describe our divine dwelling place? David describes it when he says, "The Lord is my rock, and my fortress, and my deliverer; my God, my strength, in whom I will trust; my buckler, and the horn of my salvation, and my high tower" (Psalm 18:1).

We see that our dwelling place is also our fortress, our high tower, our rock, and our refuge. We all know what a fortress is. It is a place of safety, where everything that is weak and helpless can be hidden from the enemy. We are told that God, who is our dwelling place, is also our fortress. If we live in our dwelling place, we will be perfectly safe from every assault by any enemy.

"For in the time of trouble he shall hide me in his pavilion: in the secret of his tabernacle shall he hide me; he shall set me up upon a rock" (Psalm 27:5).

"He that dwelleth in the secret place of the

Most High, shall abide under the shadow of the Almighty" (Psalm 91:1).

"Thou shalt hide them in the secret of thy presence from the pride of man: thou shalt keep them secretly in a pavilion from the strife of tongues" (Psalm 31:20).

In the secret of God's tabernacle no enemy can find us and no troubles can reach us. The "pride of man" and the "strife of tongues" find no entrance into the pavilion of God. The secret of His presence is a more secure refuge than a thousand Rocks of Gibraltar.

I do not mean that no trials will come. They may come in abundance, but they cannot penetrate the sanctuary of the soul. We may dwell in perfect peace even in the midst of life's fiercest storms.

But alas! how few of us know this. We speak David's language, but to us it is only a figure of speech. We say the things he said in the conventional, pious tone that is considered proper when speaking of religious matters.

"Oh yes, the Lord is my dwelling place. I have committed myself and all my interests to His care as every Christian ought to do."

Then one's normal conversation is resumed— "But then I cannot forget that I am a poor, good-for-nothing sort of person. I have no strength to conquer my temptations. I can hardly expect that I can be kept in the perfect security David speaks of."

Next follows a story of all sorts of fear and anxieties, exactly as if the dwelling place of God had never been heard of. It is as if the soul was wandering alone and unprotected in a world of trouble and danger.

A Picture Of The Fortress

There is a Psalm that I call the "Dwelling Place Of God." It is the Ninety-first Psalm, and it gives us a wonderful description of what this dwelling place is. "He that dwelleth in the secret place of the most high shall abide under the shadow of the Almighty. I will say of the Lord, He is my refuge and my fortress: my God; in him will I trust" (Psalm 91:1-2).

Our idea of a fortress is generally of a hard, granite building where one would be safe but, at the same time, sadly uncomfortable. There are other types of fortresses, however, that are soft, tender, and full of comfort. This Psalm describes them—"He shall cover thee with his feathers" (Psalm 91:4). Just as the mother hen covers her helpless little chickens in the fortress of her warm and brooding wings, so our God protects us in the fortress of His tender love.

The fortress of a mother's heart, whether it is of a human mother or a hen mother or a tiger mother, is the most impregnable fortress the world knows, and yet the most tender. It is this sort of a fortress that the Lord is. "Under his wings shalt thou trust" (Psalm 91:4); "He shall carry them in his bosom"

(Isaiah 40:11); "Underneath are the everlasting arms" (Deuteronomy 33:27).

Wings, bosom, arms! What blessed fortresses are these! How safe is everything that is enfolded by them.

Nature is full of such fortresses. Listen to a description of the tiger mother. "When her children are born, some power teaches the tiger to be gentle. A spirit she cannot resist, the spirit of her Creator, enters her savage heart. It is a tiger's impulse to resent an injury. Pluck her by the hair, smite her on the flank, she will leap upon and rend you. But to resent an injury is not her strongest impulse.

"Watch those impotent kitten creatures playing with her. They are so weak, a careless movement of her giant paw will destroy them; but she makes no careless movement. They have caused her a hundredfold the pain your blow produced; yet she does not render evil for evil. These puny mites of helpless impotence, she strokes with love's light in her eyes.

"She licks the shapeless forms of her tormenters. As they plunge at her, love transforms each groan of her anguish into a whinny of delight. She moves her massive head in a way which shows that He, who bade you turn the other cheek, created her. When strong enough to rise, the terrible creature goes forth to sacrifice herself for her own. She will starve that they may thrive.

She is terrible for her little ones, as God is terrible for His."

We have all seen these mother fortresses hundreds of times and have called them Godlike. One would think that the sight would have made us fly to our refuge in the dwelling place of God and leave outside all fear! But the trouble is, we refuse to believe that the Bible offers any such good news.

In effect we say, "The Lord's arms are not as dependable as the strong, loving arms of the weakest earthly mother; the Lord's bosom is not as tender as the tiger's bosom; the Lord's wings are not as brooding as the wings of the little mother hen."

We know that all these beautiful, earthly fortresses are made and fashioned by Him, but we cannot believe that He is equal to them. To have Him for our fortress does not mean to us anything half so safe or half so tender as having a mother for our fortress. And so, mothers are trusted, and God is not!

The Safest Dwelling

Yet, how safe the psalmist declares this divine dwelling place to be! "Thou shalt not be afraid for the terror by night; nor the arrow that flieth by day; nor the pestilence that walketh in darkness; nor for the destruction that wasteth at noonday. A thousand shall fall at thy side, and ten thousand at thy right hand; but it shall not come nigh thee.

Only with thine eyes shalt thou behold and see the reward of the wicked. Because thou hast made the Lord, which is my refuge, even the most High, thy habitation; There shall no evil befall thee, neither shall any plague come nigh thy dwelling" (Psalm 91:5-10).

All the terrors and all the plagues that have made our lives so uncomfortable and even so wretched, are provided for here. We will be delivered from all of them if we make the Lord our habitation.

This does not mean that we will have no outward trials. Plagues in abundance may attack your body and possessions, but these are not your inner self. Nothing can come near the interior you while you are dwelling in God.

A large part of the pain of life comes from the haunting fear of evil. Our lives are full of suppositions. Suppose this should happen, or suppose that should happen; what could we do and how could we bear it?

But if we are living in the high tower of the dwelling place of God, all these suppositions will drop out of our lives. We will be filled with peace because no threats of evil can penetrate the high tower of God. Even when walking through the valley of the shadow of death, the psalmist could say, "I will fear no evil" (Psalm 23:4). If we are dwelling in God, we can say so, too.

But you may ask how you are to get into this divine dwelling place. The answer is simply this:

124

move in. If an apartment is rented for us by a friend, and we were told the lease and all the necessary papers were duly attested and signed, we would not ask how we could get into it—we would just pack up and move in.

God says that He is our dwelling place. The Bible contains all the necessary papers, duly attested and signed. Our Lord invites us, even commands us to enter in and live there. In effect, He says, "I am your dwelling place, and you must move in."

You may ask, "But how can I move in?" You must do it by faith. God has said that He is your dwelling place. Now you must say it, too. "I will say of the Lord, He is my refuge and my fortress: my God; in him will I trust " (Psalm 91:2).

Faith reads the Word of God and believes that it is true. Christ says, "Abide." We must answer, "I will abide." Thus we make Him our habitation by faith. He is our habitation already as far as He is concerned. But we must accept Him for our dwelling place by continually asserting that He is.

We must make the eternal truth that the Lord is our dwelling place become present fact by the affirmation of our faith. We need to put on the thoughts and actions that would naturally result from having moved into the tabernacle of God.

What To Leave Behind

One of the first things we have to do is give up all worry and anxiety forever. It is unthinkable that worry and anxiety could enter the dwelling place of God; therefore, when we enter there, we must leave these undesirable possessions behind.

We talk about obeying the commands of the Lord and make a great effort in our outward observances and duties. All the while, we ignore the commands for our spiritual life, which are a thousand times more important.

"Let not your heart be troubled, neither let it be afraid" (John 14:27) is one of our Lord's commands that is almost universally disobeyed. I wonder whether our disobedience of any other command is so grievous to His heart. I know that I would be far more grieved if my child mistrusted me and felt her interests were unsafe in my care, than if in a moment of temptation she disobeyed me. I am convinced that none of us have understood how deeply it wounds the loving heart of our Lord when He finds that His people do not feel safe in His care.

We know this by our own experience. Suppose one of our friends gives us something valuable to keep for them while they are out of town. We give them every assurance that we would keep it safe. Then suppose that they go away and worry over it, as we worry about the things we commit to God. What if they express to others the same anxieties about it that we express about the things we have put into God's care?

How would we feel about it? Would we not be deeply hurt and wounded; and would we not finally be inclined to hand the thing back into our friend's own care and say, "Since it is very plain that you do not trust me, you had better take care of your things yourself."

It is amazing that God's own children can dare to be anxious after they have committed a matter to Him. It is such a slander on His trustworthiness. Unbelievers also see it in this way and think that to have the Lord for your dwelling place does not evidently amount to much after all. Otherwise, those who profess to be living there would not be so troubled.

Absolute Security

He who cares for the sparrows and numbers the hairs of our head cannot possibly fail us. He is an impregnable fortress into which no evil can enter, and no enemy can penetrate. The moment I have committed anything into this divine dwelling place is the moment that all fear and anxiety should cease. While I keep anything in my own care, I should fear and tremble, for it is indeed unsafe; but in God's care, no security could be more absolute.

The writer of Proverbs says, "The name of the Lord is a strong tower: the righteous runneth into it, and is safe" (Proverbs 18:10). The only requirement therefore is to run into this strong tower and stay there forever. It would be the height of foolishness when the enemy was surrounding us on every side to stand outside of a fortress and cry out for safety. If I want to be safe, I must go inside.

"Oh Jerusalem, Jerusalem," said our Lord, "thou that killest the prophets and stonest them which are sent unto thee, how often would I have gathered thy children together, even as a hen gathereth her chickens under her wings, and ye would not" (Matthew 23:37). If the little chick wants to be safe, it must run into the fortress of its mother's wings.

A great many people stay outside of God's dwelling place because they feel that they are too unworthy and too weak to dare to go in. What would we think of the little chick that sees the hawk coming and hears the mother calling and sees her outspread wings, but remains outside, trembling with fright? Suppose it said, "Oh, I am such a poor, weak, foolish, helpless little chicken that I am afraid I am not worthy to go under my mother's wings."

If the mother hen could speak, she would say, "You poor, foolish, little thing, it is just because you are weak and helpless and good-for-nothing that I want you under my wings. If you were a great big, strong rooster, able to take care of yourself, I would not want you at all."

Visitor Or Resident?

But we must not only run into our dwelling place. The psalmist says, "I will abide in thy tabernacle for ever: I will trust in the covert of thy wings" (Psalm 61:4). Abiding in His tabernacle forever is sometimes very hard. It is comparitively easy to take a step of faith; but it is far more difficult to live daily in God's fortress by faith. A great many people run into God's fortress on Sunday and come out of it again as soon as Monday morning dawns. Some even run into it when they kneel down to say their prayers at night and come out of it five minutes later when they get into bed. Of course, this is the height of nonsense.

One cannot imagine any sensible refugee running into a fortress one day, and the next day running out among the enemy again. We would think such a person had lost all their senses. But is it not even more foolish when it comes to our spiritual lives? Are our enemies any less active on Monday than they are on Sunday? Are we any better able to cope with them when we are in bed than when we were kneeling in prayer?

Do we want to only visit the dwelling place of God, or do we want to live there? Do we want to trust in the shelter of His wings today and tomorrow be exposed to the buffetings of our enemies outside? No one would deliberately choose the latter, but far too many drift into it. Our abiding in Christ is a matter of faith, but we fail to realize this. We think our earnest wrestlings or our strenuous efforts are a large part of the matter; and, when these slacken, our faith weakens.

The Importance Of Faith

If there is one thing that is certain, it is that the whole Christian life is to be lived by faith. Without faith it is impossible to please God. It is utterly foolish to assume that any amount of fervency or earnestness or anything of our own invention can take its place. It is useless to waste our time and energy over things that amount to nothing.

We must put all our will power and all our energy into our faith. We must "set our faces like a flint" (Isaiah 50:7) to move into the dwelling place of God. We will abide there steadfastly, despite any temptations to doubt or despair.

"He that dwelleth in the secret place of the Most High shall abide under the shadow of the Almighty." Abiding and trusting mean exactly the same thing. While I trust the Lord, I am abiding in Him. If I trust Him steadfastly, I am abiding in Him steadfastly. If I trust Him occasionally, I am running into Him and running out again.

I used to think there was some mystery about abiding in Christ, but I see now that abiding only means trusting Him fully. When you understand this, it becomes the simplest matter in the world. We sometimes say, speaking of two human beings, that they "live in each other's hearts." By this we mean that perfect love and confidence exist between them and that doubts of one another are impossible. If my trust in the fortress of the Lord is absolute, I am abiding in that fortress.

The practical thing to do since God is our Fortress and our High Tower is to surrender by faith to put ourselves and all our interests into this divine dwelling place. Then we must dismiss all care or anxiety from our minds. Since the Lord is our dwelling place, nothing can possibly come to any harm that is committed to His care.

As long as we believe this, our affairs remain in His hands. The moment we begin to doubt, we take our affairs into our own hands, and they are no longer in the divine fortress. Things cannot be in two places at once. If they are in our own care, they cannot be in God's care. And if they are in God's care, they cannot be in our own.

This is as clear as daylight, and yet, for the lack of a little common sense, people often get mixed up over it. They put their affairs into God's fortress, and at the same time put them into their own fortress as well. Then they wonder why they are not taken care of. This is all foolishness. Either trust the Lord completely or else trust yourself completely; but do not try to mix the two trusts, for they will not mix.

It often helps to put your trust into words. Say aloud, "God is my dwelling place, and I am going to abide in Him forever. It is all settled; I am in this divine habitation, and I am safe here. I am not going to move out again."

You must meet all assaults of doubt and discouragement with the simple assertion that you are in the fortress. You can affirm that you know you will not be defeated, for no one ever trusted in the Lord and was overcome. You must declare that, let other people do as they may, you are going to abide in your divine dwelling place forever. And then, having taken this stand, you must refuse to reconsider the matter. It is all settled. There is nothing more to be said about it.

I do not mean that we are to lie in bed and let things go. I am talking about the inward aspect of our affairs, not the outward. Outwardly we may have to be full of active carefulness. But the inward base of a soul must have hidden itself and all its interests in the dwelling place of God. That is what is meant by "careful for nothing" in the beautiful Bible sense of having no anxious thoughts. Be careful for nothing; but in every thing by prayer and supplication with thanksgiving let your requests be made known unto God. And the peace of God, which passeth all understanding, shall keep your hearts and minds through Christ Jesus" (Phillippians 4:6-7).

To be without care inwardly is the surest foundation for a successful Christian life. The soul that is hidden in the dwelling place of God is the soul that will be able to bear triumphantly earth's greatest trials and to conquer its strongest foes.

When we move into a new house, we not only move in ourselves, but we take with us all our belongings. Above all, we take our family. No one would be so foolish as to leave anything they cared for or anyone they loved outside. There are, however, some of God's children who move into the dwelling place of God themselves. By their lack of faith, they leave those they love best outside.

It is often their children who are so abandoned. We would be horrified at a father who, in a time of danger, fled into a fortress for safety but left his children outside. Yet, hundreds of Christians do this very thing. Every anxious thought we have about our children proves that we have not really taken them with us into the dwelling place of God.

If we trust God for our own lives, we must trust Him for our loved ones also, especially for our children. God is more their Father than their earthly father could ever be. If they are dear to us, they are far more dear to Him. We cannot do anything better than to trust them to His care. The worst thing we could do is to try to keep them in our own care.

I knew a Christian mother who trusted peacefully for her own salvation, but she was tormented with anxiety about her sons who seemed entirely indifferent to all religious subjects. One evening she heard about the possibility of putting those we love into the fortress of God by faith and leaving them there. Like a flash of heavenly light, she saw the inconsistency of hiding herself in God's fortress and leaving her beloved sons outside. At once her faith took them into the fortress with her, and she abandoned them to the care of God. So fully and completely did she do this that all her anxiety vanished and perfect peace dawned upon her soul.

She told me she felt that her sons were God's sons now. He loved them far better than she could and would care for them far more wisely and effectively. She held herself in readiness to do for them whatever the Lord might suggest. But she felt that He was the One who would know what was best, and she was content to leave the matter in His hands.

She went home from that meeting and called her sons into her room and told them what had happened. "You know my dear boys," she said, "how anxious and troubled I have been about you and how continually I have preached to you and, I am afraid, have often worried you. But now I have learned to trust, and I have put you by faith into the fortress of God. I have left you in His care. I am sure that He will care for you far better than your poor mother ever could, and He will save you in His own way. My anxieties are over."

I did not see her again for a year; but when I did, she came up to me with a beaming face. With tears of joy filling her eyes, she said, "Rejoice with me, dear friend, that I learned how to put my boys into the fortress of God. They have been safe there ever since, and all of them are good Christian boys today."

The conclusion is simply this: we must make up our minds to move into our dwelling place in God. In addition, we must take with us all our possessions, and above all, those we love. We must lose sight of everything that is outside of Him, except as we see it through His eyes. We will then see our trials as blessings and our enemies as disguised friends. We will be calm and at rest in the face of all the worries of life. "And my people shall dwell in peaceable habitation, and in sure dwellings, and in quiet resting places" (Isaiah 32:18).

Chapter 9

THE LANGUAGE OF FAITH

"But where sin abounded, grace did much more abound"—Romans 5:20.

In our preceding chapters, we have learned something about the Lord and His great salvation. What view do we take of it all? A great deal of the comfort or discomfort of our Christian lives depends on the view we take of things.

I do not mean that our view of things affects their reality in any way. But our view does make all the difference in our interpretation of this reality. While our safety comes from what things really are, our comfort comes from what we see them to be.

There is an expression used many times in the Bible to describe the salvation of the Lord Jesus Christ. It gives a view of that salvation that is so amazing and so perfectly satisfying that I wonder whether any of us have ever grasped its full meaning. One thing is certain—no one who would grasp it could ever be uncomfortable or miserable again.

It is the expression *much more*. It is used to tell us that there is no need known to man that cannot be *much more* than met by the glorious salvation that is provided.

But we are continually tempted to think that *much less* would be a truer word. Instead of this salvation being much more than our needs, it turns out in actual experience to be much less. And this *much less* view is in danger of making our whole spiritual lives miserable.

If all that we have learned in our preceding chapters of the fullness of God's salvation is indeed true, it would seem as if nothing but the language of *much more* could ever be used by any child of God. But there are some Christians who, by their thoughts and their actions, declare that they consider the language of *much less* to be the only prudent language for poor sinners. We must carefully consider the matter in the light of what the Bible tells us. Then we will discover whether we are justified in saying *much more*.

This is a far more important consideration for each one of us than it may appear at first. God declares that the salvation He has provided is much more than enough to meet our needs. If we insist on declaring in our secret thoughts that it is much less, we are casting doubt on His trustworthiness. We are also storing up for ourselves untold discomfort and misery.

While *much less* is the language of the seen things, *much more* is the language of the unseen things. Much less seems on the surface to be far more reasonable than much more, because every seen thing confirms it. Our weakness and foolishness are visible; God's strength and wisdom are invisible. Our need is evident before our eyes; God's supply is hidden in the secret of His presence and can only be realized by faith.

It seems a paradox to tell us that we must see unseen things. How can it be possible? But there are other things to see than those which appear on the surface. There are other eyes to look through than our physical eyes.

To see unseen things requires us to have that interior eye opened in our soul. This interior eye can see below the surface and pierce through the outer appearance of things into their inner realities. This interior eye looks not at the seen things, which are temporal, but at the things that are not seen, which are eternal. (See 2 Corinthians 4:18.)

The question for each one of us is whether that interior eye has been opened in us yet. Can we see the things that are eternal, or is our vision limited to the things that are temporal only? Can we say of the salvation of the Lord Jesus Christ that it is much more than our need, or that it is much less?

No Match For God

There is a wonderful instance in the history of the children of Israel, when they saw the unseen things with such clearness of vision that their enemy was powerless to disturb them. The story is told in 2 Chronicles 32:1-15.

An enemy had come up against Judah and had threatened to overwhelm them. This enemy had been so successful in all his wars with the nearby nations that he had no doubt he would be able to conquer the Israelites also. But Hezekiah, the king of Israel, looked not at the seen enemy but at the unseen God. He saw that God was the strongest.

Therefore, Hezekiah spoke comforting words to the people and said, "Be strong and courageous, be not afraid nor dismayed for the king of Assyria, nor for all the multitude that is with him, for there be more with us than with him: With him is an arm of flesh; but with us is the Lord our God to help us, and to fight our battles" (2 Chronicles 32:7-8).

What a tremendous contrast! On one side was an arm of flesh, while on the other stood the Lord our God. No wonder the people rested upon a declaration such as this. If we had been there, would we have had faith enough to rest like them?

When Sennacherib saw their faith, he was enraged. He ridiculed them for being persuaded by Hezekiah to expose themselves to the risk of death by thirst and famine. He claimed they were foolish to cling to the vain hope that the Lord would deliver them.

And then comes the taunt of the *much less*. "Know ye not," he said, "what I and my fathers have done unto all the people of other lands? were the gods of the nations of those lands any ways able to deliver their lands out of mine hand? Who was there among all the gods of those nations that my fathers utterly destroyed, that could deliver his people out of mine hand, that your God should be able to deliver you out of mine hand? Now therefore let not Hezekiah deceive you, nor persuade you on this manner, neither yet believe him: for no god of any nation or kingdom was able to deliver his people out of mine hand, and out of the land of my fathers: how much less shall your God deliver you out of mine hand" (2 Chronicles 32:13-15).

How much less—what a temptation to unbelief was shut up in those words! All the seen things were on that side. It did look impossible, especially since all the neighboring nations had been defeated. How could the nation of Israel, which was no stronger or better equipped than the others, hope to find deliverance?

But Hezekiah kept his eyes and the eyes of the people fixed on the unseen things, and their faith stood firm. The Lord in whom they trusted did not fail them, but sent them a grand deliverance. The *much less* of the enemy was turned for the Israelites into a *much more* of victory. The man who had promised them defeat and death was himself defeated. He was obliged to return to his own land with shame and was there slain by his disappointed relatives.

Trusting In God Alone

Is there any situation similar to this story in our own lives? Have we ever been taunted with the discouraging thought that God is much less than able to deliver us than His promises would lead us to expect? When we have looked at the formidable, seen things of our need, has it sometimes seemed that we were giving ourselves over to "die by famine and thirst," if we would trust in nothing else but the Lord alone? (See 2 Chronicles 32:11.)

I remember hearing of a Christian who was in great trouble, and who had tried every way for deliverance in vain. He said to a friend in a tone of the utmost despair, "Well, there is nothing left for me now but to trust the Lord."

"Alas!" exclaimed the friend in the greatest consternation, "is it possible it has come to *that?*"

We may think that we would never use such an expression. But if we are honest, we will confess that sometimes in the very bottom of our hearts, we have indulged in this same feeling. To come to the point of having nothing left to trust in but the Lord has seemed to be a desperate condition of things.

If our Lord is to be believed, His *much more's* of grace are abundantly equal to the worst emergency that can befall us. Paul tells us that God is able to do "exceeding abundantly above all that we ask or think" (Ephesians 3:20). This describes what His *much more's* mean.

We can think of very wonderful things in the way of salvation—spiritual blessings that would transform life for us and make the whole universe resplendent with joy and triumph. But do we really believe that God is able and willing to do for us exceeding abundantly above all that we can ask or think? Is the language of our hearts *much more* or *much less?*

In 1 Corinthians 2:9, we are told that "Eye hath not seen, nor ear heard, neither have entered into the heart of man, the things which God hath prepared for them that love him." God has prepared more for us than we could ever imagine. What can it be then but downright unbelief that leads us to harbor a thought of God's salvation as being less than anything that our hearts long for.

Let us settle it then that the language of our souls must be, from now on, not the *much less* of unbelief, but the *much more* of faith. We will find that God's much more's will be enough to cover the whole range of our needs, both temporal and spiritual.

"For if through the offense of one many be dead, much more the grace of God, and the gift by grace, which is by one man, Jesus Christ, hath abounded unto many" (Romans 5:15). This is a *much more* that reaches into the depth of human need.

There is no question in our minds that "many be dead," but do we believe in the *much more* of grace that is to abound to many? Are we as sure of the grace as we are of the death? Do we believe that the remedy is *much more* than the disease? Or do we believe in our hearts that it is *much less?*

One of the deepest needs of our souls is salvation. Is there a promise of *much more* available to meet this need? "But God commendeth his love toward us, in that, while we were yet sinners, Christ died for us. Much more then, being now justified by his blood, we shall be saved from wrath through him. For if, when we were enemies, we were reconciled to God by the death of his Son, much more, being reconciled, we shall be saved by his life" (Romans 5:8-10).

The question of salvation is absolutely settled by these *much more's*. Christ has died for us and has thereby reconciled us to God. If only we will let Him, He will now save us. There can be no question as to whether He will or not. The great salvation that He accomplished for us must necessarily include the lesser temporal blessings. Having done the greater, *much more* will He do the less. None of us doubt the greatness of salvation, and we dare not doubt He will take care of us daily as well.

Confidence Of Faith

Now the practical question for us in all this is— Do we really believe it? Have we rid ourselves of all doubts concerning our salvation? Can we speak with assurance of forgiveness and of eternal life? Do we say with the timidity of unbelief, "I *hope* I am a child of God;" or do we lift up our heads with joyous confidence in God as our Father and say with John, "Now *are* we the sons of God" (1 John 3:2). Is it in this respect *much more* with us or *much less?*

We long and pray for the gift of the Holy Spirit, but it seems all in vain. We feel that our prayers are not answered. But our Lord gives faith a wonderful *much more* to lay hold of for this. "If ye then, being evil, know how to give good gifts unto your children: how much more shall your heavenly Father give the Holy Spirit to them that ask him?" (Luke 11:13).

We all know how thankful and eager good parents are to give good gifts to their children. They thrust them on the child, often before he is ready to receive or even knows that he has a need. Yet, who of us believes that God is actually *much more* eager to give the Holy Spirit to them that ask Him? Is it not rather common to feel secretly that He is *much less* than willing. We think that we will have to beg, entreat, wrestle, and wait for this sorely-needed gift.

If we could only believe this *much more,* how full of faith our prayers would be. We would then be able to believe that we actually did receive that for which we asked. We would find that we were in actual possession of the Holy Spirit as our present and personal Comforter and Guide. All our weary struggles and agonizing prayers for this promised gift would be over.

Greater perhaps than any other need is our need of victory over sin and over circumstances. Like Juggernaut cars, circumstances roll over us with irresistible power and crush into the dust. The language of *much less* seems to be the only language that our souls dare speak. But God has given us a most triumphant *much more*. "For if by one man's offence death reigned by one; much more they which receive abundance of grace and of the gift of righteousness shall reign in life by one, Jesus Christ" (Romans 5:17).

We have known the reign of the spiritual death which comes by sin, and we have groaned under its power. But what do we know of that *much more* reigning in life by Jesus Christ? Do we now have greater victories than we used to have defeats? Do we reign over things much more than they once reigned over us?

It is promised in the Bible, "Nay, in all these things we are more than conquerors through him that loved us" (Romans 8:37). We have been reigned over by thousands of things—by the fear of man, by our peculiar temperaments, by our outward circumstances, by our irritable tempers, even by bad weather. We have been slaves where we ought to have been kings. We have found our reign to be *much less* rather than *much more*.

Why is this? Simply because we have not *received* enough of the abundance of grace that is ours in Christ. We have let unbelief cheat us out of our rightful possessions. We are called to be kings, and we were created to have dominion over the earth. (See Genesis 1:28.) God declares that our dominion in Christ will be *much more* powerful than our former bondage, but have we found this to be true?

God has not failed to provide the *much more* of victory. It must be that we have in some way failed to obtain it. Our failure comes because we have substituted our *much less* for God's *much more*. Deep in our hearts, we have not believed there is a sufficiency in the gift of righteousness in Christ to enable us to reign. We have failed, through our unbelief, to receive the abundance of grace that is necessary for reigning.

What is our remedy? Only this—to abandon forever our *much less* of unbelief, and to accept as true God's declaration of *much more*. We can claim at once the promised victory. According to our faith, it must and will be done for us.

Free From Care

These assurances of the *much more's* of God's salvation are not for our spiritual needs only, but for our temporal needs as well. Jesus tells us, "If God so clothe the grass of the field, which to day is, and to morrow is cast into the oven, shall he not much more clothe you, O ye of little faith?" (Matthew 6:30). To many Christians, this passage and others like it are so familiar that they have almost lost all meaning. But they do mean something almost too wonderful to believe. They tell us that God cares for us *much more* than He cares for the universe around us. He will watch over and provide for us much more than He will for His universe.

Incredible, yet true! How often we have marveled at the orderly working of the universe. We admired the great creative Power that made it and now controls it. But we never felt that it was necessary to take the burden of the universe upon our shoulders. We trusted the Creator to manage it all without our help. Yet, from the way some people find fault with the Creator's management of things, and the advice they seem to feel it necessary to give Him in their prayers, one would think the whole burden was resting upon them!

Even though we recognize that the universe is in God's care, we fail to see that we also are there. Many never dreamed that *much more* than He cares for the universe will He care for us. We have looked at the seen things of our circumstances and surroundings. We have seen the greatness of our need and our own helplessness, and we have become anxious and afraid. Instead of believing that we are of *much more* value than the fowls of the air or the lilies of the field, we live as though we are infinitely *much less*. It seems to us that the God who cares for them is not at all likely to care for us.

We say with the psalmist, "When I consider the

heavens, the work of thy fingers, the moon and the stars which thou hast ordained; What is man, that thou art mindful of him? and the son of man, that thou visitest him?'' (Psalm 8:3-4). Man is so puny, so insignificant, of so little account when compared to the great, wide universe. What is he that God should care for him?

Yet God declares that He does care for him. He even cares for him much more than He cares for the universe. Every thought of anxiety about ourselves must be immediately rejected. Since we are not so foolish as to be anxious about the universe, we must not be so much more foolish and be anxious about ourselves.

In the Sermon on the Mount, our Lord gives us the most wonderful *much more* of all. "Or what man is there of you, whom if his son ask bread, will he give him a stone? Or if he ask a fish, will he give him a serpent? If ye then, being evil, know how to give good gifts unto your children, how much more shall your Father which is in heaven give good things to them that ask him?'' (Matthew 7:11). In this *much more* we have a guarantee for the supply of every need.

All human readiness to hear and answer the child's cry of need can only be a faint picture of God's readiness; therefore, we can never dare to doubt it again. If parents would not give a stone for bread, neither would He. When we ask, we must be absolutely sure that we receive the good thing for which we asked, whether what we receive looks like it or not.

God Gives The Best

The mother of St. Augustine, in her longing for the conversion of her son, prayed that he might not go to Rome because she feared its wicked influence. God answered her by sending him to Rome to be converted there. Things we call good are often evil things. No matter how things may look, we always know that God must give the best, because He is God and could do no other.

"He that spared not his own Son, but delivered him up for us all, how shall he not with him also freely give us all things?" (Romans 8:32). Yet, we continually hear God's children lamenting their spiritual poverty and spiritual starvation. It even seems that some think it is rather a pious thing to do and a mark of true humility. This is simply glorying in the *much less* of their unbelief, instead of in the *much more* of God.

"Oh, I am such a poor creature," I heard a child of God say when urged to achieve some victory of faith. "I am such a poor creature that I cannot expect to attain to the heights you great Christians teach."

Of course you are a poor creature, and so are we all. But God is not poor. It is His part to supply your needs, not your part to supply His. God is able, no matter what unbelief may say, to "make all grace abound toward you; that ye, always having all sufficiency in all things, may abound to every good work" (2 Corinthians 9:8).

All, *always, every*—what all-embracing words these are! They include our needs to their utmost limit and leave us no room for any question. How can we, how dare we, in the face of such declarations, ever doubt or question again?

We have only touched upon the wonders of grace hidden in these *much more's* of God. We can never exhaust their meaning in this life. But let us at least resolve to lay aside every *much less* of unbelief concerning salvation. Then out of the depths of our utter weakness, sinfulness, and need, let us assert with a conquering faith, always and everywhere, the mighty *much more* of the grace of God.

Chapter 10

JESUS—THE CENTER OF OUR ATTENTION

"Examine yourselves, whether ye be in the faith"—2 Corinthians 13:5.

Probably no subject connected with the Christian life has been the cause of more discomfort and suffering to tender consciences than this subject of self-examination. Nothing has led more frequently to the language of *much less,* which in our last chapter we found to be a great obstacle to all spiritual growth.

It has been constantly impressed upon us that it is our duty to examine ourselves. The eyes of most of us are continually turned inward. Our gaze is fixed on our interior states and feelings to such an extent that self, not Christ, has come to fill the whole picture. By *self* I mean all that centers around this great big *Me* of ours. Its vocabulary rings out with "I," "me," and "my."

The question we ask ourselves in our times of self-examination are proof of this. Am I earnest enough? Have I repented enough? Do I have the right sort of feelings? Do I understand religious truth as I should? Are my prayers fervent enough? Is my interest in spiritual things as great as it should be? Do I love God with enough fervor? Is the Bible as much of a delight to me as it is to others?

All these and a hundred more questions about ourselves and our experiences fill our thoughts and sometimes our little self-examination books as well. Day and night we ring out the changes on the personal pronoun I, me, my, to the utter exclusion of any thought concerning Christ, or any word such as He, His, Him.

The misery of this tendency is known by many of us. But the idea that the Bible is full of commands for self-examination is so prevalent that it seems one of the most truly pious things we can do. As miserable as it makes us, we still feel it is our duty to go on with it, in spite of an ever-increasing sense of hopelessness and despair.

Scriptural Self-Examination

Many will be surprised to find that there are only two texts in the whole Bible that speak of self-examination. Neither of these can be interpreted to approve of the morbid self-analysis that results from what we call self-examination.

"Examine yourselves, whether ye be in the faith." This is simply an exhortation to the Corinthians, who were in a sadly backslidden condition, to settle definitely whether they were still believers or not.

"Examine yourselves whether you be in the *faith*." It does not say examine whether you are sufficiently earnest or whether your motives are pure; it only says, "whether you are in the faith." In short, do you believe in Christ or not? It is a simple question that requires only a straightforward answer, yes or no. This is what it meant for the Corinthians then, and it is what it means for us now.

The other passage reads, "Wherefore whosoever shall eat this bread, and drink this cup of the Lord, unworthily, shall be guilty of the body and blood of the Lord. But let a man examine himself, and so let him eat of that bread, and drink of that cup" (2 Corinthians 11:27-28).

Paul was writing here of the abuses of greediness and drunkenness which had crept in at the celebration of the Lord's Supper. In this exhortation to examine themselves, he was urging them to see to it that they did none of these things, but rather to partake of this religious feast in a decent and orderly manner.

Neither of these passages hint at the searching out of one's emotions and experiences that we call self-examination. It is amazing that out of two such simple passages a teaching evolved that brought so much misery to earnest souls.

The truth is, there is no Scriptural authority for this disease of modern times. Those who are afflicted with it are the victims of mistaken ideas of God's ways with His children.

You may be asking whether I have not overlooked a large number of passages that tell us to *watch*. You may wonder whether these passages mean watching ourselves, or in other words, self-examination. I will quote one of these passages as a sample, that we may see what the true meaning is.

"But of that day and that hour knoweth no man, no, not the angels which are in heaven, neither the Son, but the Father. Take ye heed, watch and pray: for ye know not when the time is. For the Son of man is as a man taking a far journey, who left his house, and gave authority to his servants, and to every man his work, and commanded the porter to watch. Watch ye therefore: for ye know not when the master of the house cometh, at even, or at midnight, or at the cockcrowing, or in the morning: Lest coming suddenly he find you sleeping. And what I say unto you I say unto all, Watch" (Mark 13:32-37).

If we examine this passage and others like it carefully, we will see that, instead of teaching self-examination, they teach something that is exactly the opposite. They tell us to *watch,* it is true, but they do not tell us to watch ourselves. Rather, they command us to forget ourselves in watching for Another.

The return of the Lord is the thing we are to watch for. His coming footsteps and not our own past footsteps are to be the object of our gazing. We are to watch as a servant watches for the return of the master of the house. We are to be ready as a good watchman should be, to receive and welcome Him at any moment that He appears.

Looking To Him

"Blessed are those servants, whom the lord when he cometh shall find watching" (Luke 12:37). Are they to be watching themselves? No, they should be watching for Him, of course.

Imagine a servant who, instead of watching for the return of his master, spent his time dejectedly analyzing his own past conduct, trying to discover whether he had been faithful enough. Suppose he became so absorbed in self-examination that he let the master's call go unheeded and the master's return unnoticed. This is a picture of what the soul experiences when it becomes absorbed in the wrong habit of watching and looking at self, instead of watching and looking at Christ.

These passages, therefore, instead of teaching self-examination, teach exactly the opposite. God says, "Look unto me, and be saved" (Isaiah 45:22). But the self-analyzing soul says, "I must look unto myself if I am to have any hope of being saved. It must be by getting myself right that salvation is to come."

The phrase "Looking unto Jesus" is generally acknowledged to be one of the watchwords of the Christian faith. All Christians will unhesitatingly declare that, of course, this is the one thing we all should do. But after saying this, they will go on in their old way of introspection, trying to find some salvation in their own feelings or in their own works of righteousness. Then they feel depressed because they never find it.

It is obvious that we see what we look at and cannot see what we look away from. We cannot look at Jesus while we are looking at ourselves. The power for victory and endurance comes from looking to Jesus and considering Him. Certainly, no power comes from looking to or considering ourselves or our circumstances, sins, or temptations.

All that looking at ourselves causes is weakness and defeat. This is because when we look at ourselves we see nothing but our own weakness, poverty, and sin. We cannot see the remedy for these and, as a matter of course, we are defeated. The remedy was there for us all the time. But it is not found where we are looking, for it is not in self but in Christ. We must decide whether we will turn our backs on Christ and look at ourselves, or turn our backs on self and look at Christ.

The Christian author Adelaide Proctor suggested, "For one look at self take ten looks at Christ." This simple statement carried conviction to my soul and delivered me from a habit of self-examination and introspection that had made me miserable for years. It was an unspeakably wonderful deliverance. My experience since that time leads me to believe that even a better motto would be, "Take no looks at self at all, but look only and always at Christ."

Eliminating The Old Man

The Biblical law regarding the self-life is not that the self-life must be watched and made better. Rather, it must be put off.

"That ye put off concerning the former conversation the old man, which is corrupt according to the deceitful lusts" (Ephesians 4:22).

The old man is of course the self-life. This self-life (which we know only too well is corrupt according to deceitful lusts) is not to be improved, but to be put off. It is to be crucified. Paul says that our old man is crucified or put to death with Christ. "Lie not one to another, seeing that ye have put off the old man with his deeds" (Colossians 3:9).

Some people's ideas of crucifying the old man is to set him up against a wall, and then throw darts at him to make him miserable, keeping him alive all the time. But crucifixion means death. To crucify the old man means to kill him outright and to discard him as a snake discards its dead and useless skin.

It is useless then for us to examine self and to tinker with it, in the hope of improving it. The Lord wants us to get rid of it. Fenelon, in his "Spiritual Letters," says that the only way to treat self is to refuse to have anything to do with it. He says we must turn our backs on this great big *I* of ours and say to it, "I do not know you and am not interested in you, and I refuse to pay any attention to you whatever."

But self is always determined to secure attention. It would rather be thought badly of than not to be thought of at all. Self-examination, with all its miseries, often gives a sort of morbid satisfaction to the self-life in us. It even deludes self into thinking it is a very humble and pious sort of self after all.

The only safe and Scriptural way is to have nothing to do with self at all, either good self or bad self. It is much better simply to ignore self and to fix our eyes, thoughts, and expectations on the Lord alone. We must substitute the personal pronouns *I, me,* and *my,* with the pronouns *He, Him,* and *His.* We must not ask ourselves, "Am I good?" Rather, we should ask, "Is He good?"

Unravelling Life's Snarls

The psalmist says, "Mine eyes are ever toward the Lord; for he shall pluck my feet out of the net" (Psalm 25:15). As long as our eyes are toward our feet and toward the net in which they are entangled, we only get into worse tangles. But when we keep our eyes on the Lord, He plucks our feet out of the net.

I have found this to be true through many personal experiences. No matter what sort of a difficulty I may have been in, when I kept my eyes on the problem and tried to unravel it, it grew worse. But when I turned my eyes away from the problem and kept them fixed on the Lord, He always unraveled it and delivered me.

Have you ever watched a farmer plowing a field? In order to make straight furrows, he must fix his eyes on a tree or a post in the fence or some object at the far side of the field. He then will guide his plow unwaveringly toward the object. If he begins to look behind him to see whether he has made a straight furrow, his plow begins to jerk from side to side. As a result, the furrow he is making becomes a zigzag.

If we want to make straight paths for our feet, we must do what Paul says he did, "Forgetting those things which are behind, and reaching forth unto those things which are before, I press toward the mark for the prize of the high calling of God in Christ Jesus" (Philippians 3:13-14). To forget the things that are behind is an essential part of pressing forward toward the prize of our high calling. This prize can never be reached unless we forget the past. When we do, we put an end to all our self-examination because if we do not look back over our past misdoings, we will find little food for self-reflection.

We complain of spiritual hunger and torment ourselves by wondering why our hunger is not satisfied. The psalmist says, "The eyes of all wait upon thee; and thou givest them their meat in due season" (Psalm 145:15). Having our eyes upon ourselves and on our own hunger will never bring a supply of spiritual meat.

To examine self is to be like a man who spends his time examining his empty refrigerator instead of going to the market for food. No wonder so many Christians are starving to death in the midst of all the fullness there is for them in Christ. They never see that fullness, because they never look at it.

Somehow, people lay aside their common sense when they come to the subject of spiritual things. They expect to see things from which they have deliberately kept their backs turned. They cry out, "O Lord, reveal Yourself." Then instead of looking at Him, they keep their gaze fixed on their own inward feelings. They wonder at the mysterious dealings of God in hiding His face from their fervent prayers. But how can they see what they do not look at?

It is never God who hides His face from us. We turn our faces from Him. "For they have turned their back unto me, and not their face" (Jeremiah 2:27).

When Christians spend their time examining their own condition, listing all their sins, and bemoaning their shortcomings, they are setting up their own sinful self upon the chief pedestal in their hearts. They are making it the center of their whole religious life and of all their care and efforts. They gaze at the great, big, miserable self until it fills their whole horizon. At the same time, they turn their backs on the Lord, until they lose sight of Him completely.

We are never commanded to behold our emotions or our experiences or even our sins. But we are commanded to turn our backs upon all these and to behold the Lamb of God who takes away our sins. One look at Christ is worth more for salvation than a million looks at self. Yet, we think that the humility which results from self-examination must have in it some saving power because it makes us so miserable. We have to travel a long way on our heavenly journey before we fully learn that there is no saving power in misery. A cheerful, confident faith is the only successful attitude for the believer's soul.

God's Chosen Fast

In Isaiah we see God's people complaining that they fasted, and He did not see. They afflicted their souls, and He did not notice. God gave them this significant answer, "Is it such a fast that I have chosen? a day for a man to afflict his soul? is it to bow down his head as a bulrush, and to spread sackcloth and ashes under him? wilt thou call this a fast, and an acceptable day to the Lord?" (Isaiah 58:5).

Whoever else may be pleased with the miseries of our self-examination, it is very certain that God is not. He calls upon us, as He did upon His people of old, to forget our own miserable selves and to go to work to lessen the miseries of others.

"Is not this the fast that I have chosen?" He says, "To loose the bands of wickedness, to undo the heavy burdens, and to let the oppressed go free, and that ye break every yoke? Is it not to deal thy bread to the hungry, and that thou bring the poor that are cast out to thy house? when thou seest the naked, that thou cover him?" (Isaiah 58:6-7).

Service for others is of infinitely greater value to the Lord than the longest sessions of self-examination and self-abasement. He shows us the surest way of deliverance out of the mire of misery, into which our habits of self-examination have plunged us. We need to give up our own "fast" of afflicting our souls and bowing down our heads. "And if thou draw out thy soul to the hungry, and satisfy the afflicted soul; then shall thy light rise in obscurity, and thy darkness be as the noonday: And the Lord shall guide thee continually, and satisfy thy soul in drought, and make fat thy bones: and thou shalt be like a watered garden, and like a spring of water, whose waters fail not" (Isaiah 58:10-11).

All this is exactly what we have been striving after, but our strivings have been in our own way, not in God's. The fast we have chosen has been to afflict our souls, to bow down our heads, and to sit in sackcloth and ashes. Instead of our bones being made fat and our souls refreshed like a watered garden, we have found only hunger, thirst, and misery. Our own fasts, no matter how fervently they may be carried on or how many groans and tears may accompany them, can never bring us anything else.

Now let us try God's fast. Let us lay aside all care for ourselves and care instead for our needy brothers and sisters. Let us stop trying to do something for our own poor, miserable self-life and try to do something to help the spiritual lives of others. Let us give up our hopeless efforts to find something in ourselves to delight in. Instead, let us delight ourselves only in the Lord and in His service. If we will do this, all the days of our misery will be ended.

Some may ask whether it is necessary to examine ourselves in order to find out what is wrong and what needs mending. But since we are God's workmanship, He is the One to examine us. He is the only One who can tell us what is wrong.

The man who makes watches is the one to examine a watch when it is out of order. We have too much sense to meddle with our watches. Why is it that we do not have enough good sense to give up meddling with our lives?

Surely we must see that the examining of the Lord is the only kind of examination that is of any use. His examination is like that of a physician who examines in order to cure. Our self-examination is like that of the patient who becomes more of a hypochondriac as he continues to examine the symptoms of his disease.

Dealing With Sin

When there has been actual sin, should there be self-examination and self-reproach, at least for a time? This is a fallacy which deceives a great many Christians. It seems too much to believe that we can be forgiven without first going through a season of self-reproach.

But what does the Bible teach? John tells us, "If we confess our sins" (not bewail them or try to excuse them), "he is faithful and just to forgive us our sins, and to cleanse us from all unrighteousness" (1 John 1:9).

All that God wants is for us to turn to Him at once, acknowledge our sins, and believe in His forgiveness. Every minute that we delay in order to spend the time in self-reproach only adds further sin to that which we have already committed. If ever we need to look away from self and have our eyes turned to the Lord, it is when we become conscious of having sinned against Him.

All through the Bible we are taught this lesson of death to self and life in Christ alone. "Not I, but Christ" was not intended to be a unique experience of the apostle Paul, but should be the experience of every Christian.

We sing sometimes, "Thou, O Christ, art all I want," but we truly want a great many other things. We want good feelings; we want fervor and earnestness. We want realizations, and we want satisfying experiences. And we continually examine ourselves to try to find out why we do not have these things. We think if we could only discover our points of failure, we would be able to set them straight.

But there is no healing or transforming power in gazing at our failures. The only road to Christlikeness is to behold, not our own sinfulness, but His goodness and beauty. We grow like what we look at. If we spend our lives looking at our sinful selves, we will become more and more sinful.

Dangers Of Self-Reflection

Self-examination always seems to make us worse instead of better. As we gaze at self, we are changed into the image of self. We can instead spend our time beholding the glory of the Lord. As we let our minds dwell upon His goodness and love and drink in His Spirit, we will be, slowly perhaps but surely, changed into the image of the Lord upon whom we are gazing.

Fenelon says that we should never indulge in any self-reflective acts, either of disappointment at our failures or of congratulation at our successes. Rather, we should continually commit self and all self's doings to oblivion and keep our interior eyes upon the Lord only. It is very hard in self-examination not to try to find excuses for our faults. Our self-reflective acts are often in danger of being turned into self-glorifying ones. The only way is to ignore self altogether and to forget there is any such being in existence.

I have known Christian workers whose lives have been one long torment because of these self-reflective acts. The "Blue Mondays," which so many clergymen complain about, are the result of an indulgence in self-reflective acts concerning their church services the day before.

The only way to treat all forms of self-reflective acts is simply to give them up. They always do harm and never good. They are bound to result in one of two things: either they fill us full of self-praise and self-satisfaction or they plunge us into the depths of discouragement and despair. In any case, the soul is shut out from any sight of God and of His salvation.

An effective way of conquering the habit is to make a rule that whenever we are tempted to examine ourselves, we will immediately begin to examine the Lord instead. Then we will let thoughts of His love and His all-sufficiency sweep out all thoughts of our own unworthiness and helplessness.

When we set the Lord before our eyes in all the beauty of His character and His ways, the sight will be so lovely that it will take our eyes off everything else. But no revelation of God will be of any use if we will not look at it. We can do no good if we persist in turning our backs on what has been revealed and gaze instead at our own inward experiences. I must repeat that we cannot see self and see the Lord at the same time. While we are examining self, we cannot be looking at Him.

Fenelon says this concerning self-examination: "There is something very hidden and very deceptive in the suffering it causes; for while you seem to yourself to be wholly occupied with the glory of God, in your inmost soul it is self alone that occasions all your trouble. You are indeed desirous that God should be glorified, but you wish it should take place by means of your perfection, and you thus cherish the sentiments of self-love. It is simply a refined pretext for dwelling in self."

Fenelon goes on to say, "It is a sort of infidelity to simple faith when we desire to be continually assured that we are doing well. It is, in fact, a desire to know what we are doing, which we shall never know, and of which it is the will of God we should be ignorant. It is trifling by the way, in order to reason about the way. The safest and shortest course is to renounce, forget, and abandon self, and, through faithfulness to God, to think no more of it. This is the whole of religion—to get out of self and self-love, in order to get into God."

What we must do, therefore, is to shut the door resolutely and forever upon self and all of self's experiences, whether they are good or bad. We must say with the psalmist, "I have set the Lord always before me: because he is at my right hand, I shall not be moved. Therefore my heart is glad, and my glory rejoiceth: my flesh also shalt rest in hope" (Psalm 16:8-9).

Chapter 11

THINGS THAT CANNOT BE SHAKEN

"And this word, Yet once more, signifieth the removing of those things that are shaken, as of things that are made, that those things which cannot be shaken may remain"—Hebrews 12:27.

After all that we have considered of the depth of the love and care of God, those who do not understand His ways may get the wrong impression. They may assume that no trials or difficulties could ever come into the lives of His children. But often, love itself must bring the hard times.

"For whom the Lord loveth he chasteneth, and scourgeth every son whom he receiveth. If ye endure chastening, God dealeth with you as with sons; for what son is he whom the father chasteneth not? But if ye be without chastisement, whereof all are partakers, then are ye bastards, and not sons" (Hebrews 12:6-8).

If love sees those it loves going wrong, it must, because of love, do what it can to save them. The love that fails to do this is only selfish. Likewise, when the God of love sees His children resting their souls on things that can be shaken, He must remove those things from their lives. Then they will be driven to rest only on the things that cannot be shaken. This process of removal is sometimes very hard.

Everlasting Foundations

If our souls are to rest in peace and comfort, it can only be on unshakable foundations. It is no more possible for the soul to be comfortable when it is trying to rest on things that can be shaken than it is for the body to rest comfortably in a shaking bed.

For foundations to be reliable, they must always be unshakable. A house built on the sand may look fine in clear and sunny weather. But when storms arise and the winds blow and floods come, that house will fall. On the contrary, the house built on the rock is able to withstand all the stress of the storm and remains unshaken through wind and floods, for it is founded on the rock. (See Matthew 7:24-27.)

It is very possible in the Christian life to build one's spiritual house on insecure foundations. When storms beat upon it, the ruin of that house will be great. Many religious experiences seem genuine when all goes well in life. But when trials come, faith totters and falls because its foundations are insecure. It is, therefore, of vital importance to see to it that our spiritual life is built upon things that cannot be shaken.

Of course, the immediate thought that will come to every mind is that our faith must be built upon the rock, Christ Jesus. This is certainly true. But we need to learn what is really meant by that expression. It is one of those religious phrases that is often used with no definite or real meaning attached to it.

Traditionally, we believe that Christ is the only Rock upon which to build. But, perhaps unconsciously, we believe that many other things must be added to Christ. We think that the right feelings must be added or the right doctrines or dogmas or whatever else seems to measure up to the necessary degree of security. If we were perfectly honest with ourselves, we would often find that we depend almost completely upon these additions of our own. Christ Himself, as our Rock of dependence, becomes of secondary importance.

When we talk of building upon the Rock Christ Jesus, we should realize that the Lord is enough for our salvation. Without any additions of our own, the Lord Himself, as He is in His own character, our Creator and Redeemer, is our all-sufficient portion.

The Necessity Of Shaking

The "foundation of God standeth sure," and it is

the only foundation that does. Therefore, we need to be shaken off of every other foundation in order that we may be forced to rest on the foundation of God alone. This explains the necessity for those shakings through which so many Christians pass.

The Lord sees that we are building our spiritual houses on flimsy foundations which will not be able to withstand the storms of life. In tenderest love, He shakes our earth and our heaven until all that can be shaken is removed, and only those things which cannot be shaken are left behind.

Paul tells us that the things that are shaken are the "things that are made." These are things manufactured by our own efforts, feelings that we work up, doctrines that we invent, and good works that we perform. It is not that these are bad things in themselves. It is only when the soul begins to rest on them instead of upon the Lord that He is compelled to shake us from them. This shaking applies not to the earth only, but also to heaven. It is possible to have "things that are made" even in religious matters.

Much of the so-called religiousness of many Christians consists of these "things that are made." Perhaps the great overturnings and tossings in matters of faith which so distress Christians may be the necessary shaking of the "things that are made." Then, only that which cannot be shaken may remain.

There are times in our Christian lives when our faith seems to be as settled and immoveable as the roots of the everlasting mountains. But then comes an upheaval, and all our foundations are shaken and thrown down. We are ready to despair and question whether we can be Christians at all.

Sometimes it is an upheaval in our outward circumstances, and sometimes it is in our inward experiences. If people have rested on their good works and their faithful service, the Lord is often obliged to take away all power or opportunity for work. The soul is driven from its false resting place and forced to rest in the Lord alone.

Sometimes the dependence is upon good feelings or pious emotions. The soul has to be deprived of these before it can learn to depend only upon God. Sometimes the believer depends upon what he believes to be sound doctrine. He feels that he is occupying an invulnerable position because his views are so correct and his doctrines are so orthodox. Then the Lord is obliged to shake his doctrines and to plunge him into confusion and darkness about his views. Then, that which looks like certain spiritual ruin and defeat can be turned into the most triumphant victory by the Lord.

The upheaval may come in our outward circumstances. Everything seems so firmly established in prosperity that no dream of disaster disturbs us. Our reputation is assured, our work has prospered, our efforts have all been successful beyond our hopes, and our soul is at ease. The need for God is in danger of becoming far off and vague.

Then the Lord is obliged to put an end to it all. Our prosperity crumbles around us like a house built on the sand. We are tempted to think He is angry with us. But in truth, it is not anger, but tenderest love. His love compels Him to take away the outward prosperity that is keeping our souls from entering into the interior spiritual Kingdom of which we long to be part.

"Although the fig tree shall not blossom, neither shall fruit be in the vines; the labour of the olive shall fail, and the fields shall yield no meat; the flock shall be cut off from the fold, and there shall be no herd in the stalls: Yet I will rejoice in the Lord, I will joy in the God of my salvation" (Habakkuk 3:17-18).

Paul declared, "I count all things but loss. . .that I may win Christ" (Philippians 3:8). When we learn to say the same, the peace and joy that the gospel promises becomes ours.

Sweeping Away False Refuges

"What iniquity," asks the Lord of the children of Israel, "have your fathers found in me, that they are gone far from me, and have walked after vanity. . .For my people have committed two evils; they have forsaken me the fountain of living waters, and hewed them out cisterns, broken cisterns, that can hold no water" (Jeremiah 2:5,13).

Like the Israelites, we too forsake the fountain of living waters and try to dig out for ourselves cisterns of our own devising. We seek to cool our thirst with our own experiences or our own activities. Then we wonder why we still thirst. To save us from perishing for lack of water, the Lord destroys our broken cisterns. He does it only so can we be forced to drink from the fountain of living waters.

We are told that if we trust in vanity, vanity will be our reward. It is like crossing a dangerous swamp abounding in quicksand, where every step is dangerous. Firm looking mounds of earth will cause you to sink in the mire and water concealed below if you trust their deceptive appearances.

This is what it means to "trust in vanity." As you discover the rottenness of your false dependences, you will learn to trust in that which is safe and permanent.

"I waited patiently for the Lord; and he inclined unto me, and heard my cry. He brought me up also out of an horrible pit, out of the miry clay, and set my feet upon a rock, and established my goings. And he hath put a new song in my mouth, even praise unto our God: many shall see it, and fear, and shall trust in the Lord" (Psalm 40:1-3).

Sweeping Away False Refuges

The prophet Isaiah lamented the sins of his people. He said, "We have made lies our refuge, and under falsehoods have we hid ourselves" (Isaiah 28:15). The Lord had declared, "The hail shall sweep away the refuge of lies, and the waters shall overflow the hiding place" (Isaiah 28:17).

It might look as though it was God's wrath that did this. Many frightened Christians think that it is. But His wrath is only against the refuges of lies, not against us. Love could do no less than destroy these refuges in order that we may be delivered.

The soul is continually tempted to sit down on some false idea as though it was a final resting place. God is continually obliged to remove all such false resting places as one would remove the seat of a chair. At last, the soul will settle down upon the only true rest in God. This removal is only another word for shakings and emptyings.

It is always a painful process and often a most discouraging one. No sooner do we find an experience or a doctrine in which we think we may surely rest, than a great shaking comes. We are forced out again. This process continues until all that can be shaken is removed, and only those things which cannot be shaken remain.

Often the answer to our most fervent prayers for deliverance comes in a form that seems to shake the foundations of our being. Through this shaking, the deliverance for which we prayed is accomplished. Through it all, we will be brought forth into the secure place for which we long.

Detached From The World

The old Bible teachers used to lecture on what they called *detachment*. This referred to cutting the soul loose from all that could hold it back from God. This need for detachment is the reason for many of our shakings. We cannot follow the Lord fully as long as we are tied tightly to anything else. It would be like a boat trying to sail out into the boundless ocean while it is tied fast to the shore.

If we want to reach the "city which hath foundations" spoken of in Hebrews 11, we must go out like Abraham from all other cities. We must be detached from every earthly tie. Everything in Abraham's life that could be shaken was shaken. He was emptied from vessel to vessel, here today and gone tomorrow. All his resting places were disturbed, and no settlement or comfort could be found anywhere.

We, like Abraham, are looking for "a city which hath foundations, whose builder and maker is God" (Hebrews 11:10). We too will need to be emptied from vessel to vessel. Often, we do not realize this. When the shakings come, we are in despair and think we will never reach that city. Actually, it is these very shakings that make it possible for us to reach it.

The psalmist had learned this divine principle. After all the shakings of his eventful life, he cried, "My soul, wait thou only upon God; for my expectation is from him. He only is my rock and my salvation: he is my defence; I shall not be moved. In God is my salvation and my glory: the rock of my strength, and my refuge, is in God" (Psalm 62:5-7). At last God was everything to him; and then he found that God was enough.

It is the same with us. Everything in our lives and experience may be shaken, and only that which cannot be shaken remains. We are brought to see that God only is our rock and our foundation. We learn to have our expectation from Him alone.

"Therefore will not we fear, though the earth be removed, and though the mountains be carried into the midst of the sea; Though the waters thereof roar and be troubled, though the mountains shake with the swelling thereof. . . .God is in the midst of her; she shall not be moved: God shall help her, and that right early" (Psalm 46:2-3).

"Shall not be moved"—what an inspiring declaration! We are so easily moved by the things of earth. Can we possibly arrive at a place where nothing can upset our temper or disturb our calm? Yes, we can.

The apostle Paul knew the place of perfect peace. When he was on his way to Jerusalem, he knew that bonds and afflictions awaited him. In spite of this, he could say triumphantly, "But none of these things move me" (Acts 20:24).

Everything in Paul's life and experience that could be shaken had been shaken. He no longer counted his life or any of life's possessions as dear to him. If we let God have His way with us, we will come to the same place. Neither the worries of the little things of life, nor its great and heavy trials can move us from the peace that passes all understanding. This is the benefit of those who have learned to rest only on God.

In that wonderful Revelation made to John on the Isle of Patmost the Spirit tells the churches what awaits those who overcome. "Him that overcometh will I make a pillar in the temple of my God, and he shall go no more out" (Revelation 3:12). To be as unmoveable as a pillar in the house of our God would cause one to gladly endure all the shakings necessary to bring us there!

"Wherefore we receiving a kingdom which cannot be moved, let us have grace, whereby we may serve God acceptably with reverence and godly fear: For our God is a consuming fire" (Hebrews 12:28-29). A great many people are afraid of the consuming fire of God. That is only because they do not understand what it is. The fire of God's love must consume everything that can harm His people. If our hearts are set on being what the love of God would have us to be, His fire is something we will not be afraid of, but warmly welcome instead.

Refined Like Silver

The consuming fire of God's love will not cease to burn until it has refined us as silver is refined. "And he shall sit as a refiner and purifier of silver: and he shall. . .purge them as gold and silver, that they may offer unto the Lord an offering in righteousness" (Malachi 3:3). If we submit to this purifying process, we will become pleasant to the

Lord. All nations shall call us blessed, "for ye shall be a delightsome land, saith the Lord of Hosts" (Malachi 3:12).

To be pleasant and delightsome to the Lord may seem impossible when we look at our shortcomings and unworthiness. But when we think of this lovely consuming fire of God's love, we can be of good cheer and take courage. He will not fail or be discouraged until all our dross is burned up, and we come forth in His likeness.

Our souls long for the Kingdom which cannot be moved. God will, if we let Him, shake everything in our lives that can be shaken. He will push us off of every false rest. Finally, only that which cannot be shaken will remain.

One of the most impressive sermons I ever heard was preached by a sweet old Quaker lady. She rose in the stillness of the meeting and said, "Yesterday sister Tabitha broke all to pieces my best china teapot, but the Lord, whom I trust, kept my soul in perfect peace, and enabled me not to utter a single word of reproach."

That was all; the sermon was ended. But into every heart there entered a sense of what it would mean to be kept in the immoveable Kingdom of the love of God.

This Kingdom may be our home. We must submit to the shakings of God and learn to rest only and always on Him.

May He hasten the day for each one of us!

Chapter 12

A WORD TO THE WAVERING ONES

"But let him ask in faith, nothing wavering. For he that wavereth is like a wave of the sea driven with the wind and tossed. For let not that man think that he shall receive anything of the Lord"—James 1:6-7.

It would be difficult to find anything that produces more discomfort in the Christian life than wavering faith. The illustration given us by James describes it exactly—"a wave of the sea driven by the wind and tossed." It is impossible for a traveler to reach his destination by advancing one day and retracing his steps the next. It is equally impossible for the wavering soul to reach any place of settled peace.

In our last chapter we considered the shakings of God. We may think that our waverings are related to His shakings. But God's shakings are caused by His love and are for our blessing. They always lead to rest and peace. Our waverings are caused by our lack of faith and always lead to discomfort and turmoil.

A wavering Christian is a Christian who trusts in the love of God one day and doubts it the next. He mounts to the hilltop of joy, only to descend into the valley of despair. He is driven to and fro by every wind of doctrine and is always striving and never attaining. He is a prey to each changing influence caused by his state of health or by his circumstances or even by the weather.

Even the most ignorant child of God should know that this sort of experience is all wrong. To waver in one's faith is most dishonoring to the Lord. It slanders the truth and faithfulness of His nature.

Many Christians' eyes are so blinded that they actually think this tendency to waver is a tribute to the humility of their spirits. They exalt every fresh attack of doubt into a secret and most pious virtue. A wavering Christian will say complacently, "Oh, but I know that I am so unworthy. I am sure it is right for me to doubt." They will imply by their tone of superiority that if you were truly humble, you would doubt also.

I knew one devoted Christian whose religious life was one long torment of doubt. He said to me once in solemn earnestness, after I had been urging him to have more faith, "My dear friend, if once I should be so presumtuous as to feel sure that God loved me, I should be certain I was on the direct road to hell." He thought that such an assurance could only arise from a feeling that he was good enough to be worthy of God's love.

For us to think that we are good enough to be worthy of God's love would be presumption indeed. But our assurance does not come from our own goodness, but from the goodness of God. We never can be and never should be satisfied with our own goodness. There cannot possibly be any question, however, to one who believes the Bible, concerning the all-sufficiency of the goodness of God.

To see the absurdity of the doubt of this dear Christian, we can consider how it would affect any of our human relationships. Suppose a wife or husband had a wavering confidence in the other, one day trusting, and the next day doubting. Would this be a sign of true humility on the doubter's part? Would it be cherished as a virtue? Suppose the children waver in their confidence toward their earthly parents as Christians often do with their heavenly Parent. What words would be severe enough to describe such unacceptable conduct?

In earthly relationships such wavering might occur because someone was unworthy of confidence. In this case it could be excused. But in the case of God, there could not possibly be any such excuse. The wavering faith of some of His children lead unbelievers to conclude that God cannot be worthy of much confidence.

We would not want to be the cause of any such

doubt of the goodness of God. Our wavering faith gives just such an impression however. It is nothing less than disloyalty to a trustworthy God, and it should be mourned over as a grievous sin.

Receiving And Keeping Blessings

Our wavering comes from a subtle and often unconscious form of pride. True humility accepts the love that is bestowed upon it. It receives the gifts of that love with a meek and happy thankfulness. Pride shrinks from accepting gifts and kindness. It is afraid to believe in the pure motives and goodness of the one who bestows them.

If we were truly humble, we would accept God's love with thankful meekness. We would still acknowledge our own unworthiness, but we would only think of it as enhancing His grace and goodness in choosing us as the recipients of such blessings.

A wavering faith is not only disloyal to God. It is also a source of untold misery to ourselves as well. It cannot advance our spiritual interests, but it always hinders and upsets them. The apostle Paul tells us that we are made partakers of Christ if we "hold the beginning of our confidence steadfast unto the end" (Hebrews 3:14).

To be steadfast is the opposite of wavering. To expect steadfastness to come as the result of wavering is foolishness. It is like expecting to reach the top of a mountain by alternating short climbs up with long and disastrous slides down.

Yet, many people expect this very thing. They make a beginning of confidence. While the freshness of it lasts, they are full of joy and triumph. Then trials and temptations come. Doubts begin to intrude. Instead of treating these doubts as enemies to be resisted and driven away, they receive them as friends and give them entertainment. Sooner or later they begin to waver in their faith. All settled peace is gone. When skies are bright and all goes well with them, their faith flourishes. But when skies are dark and things go wrong, doubts triumph, and they waver again.

Mountain Climbing

I once had a conversation with a clergyman on the possibility of a spiritual life of constant peace and rest. He told me frankly that he did not believe it was possible. He thought that most Christian experience was like his own.

When I want to write my sermons, he said, "I get up on the mountaintop by prayer and by climbing. I put my foot first on one promise and then on another. By hard climbing and much praying, I reach the summit and can begin my sermon. All goes fine for a little while. Then suddenly an interruption comes, some trouble with my children or some domestic upset in the house or some quarrel with a neighbor, and down I tumble from the mountaintop. I can only get back again by another exhausting climb.

"Sometimes," he said, "I stay on the summit for

two or three days, and once in a great while, even for two or three weeks. But as to there being any possibility of being seated in heavenly places in Christ and abiding there continually, I cannot believe it."

This describes the experience of many of God's children who are hungering and thirsting for the peace and rest that Christ has promised them. They always seem unable to obtain it for more than a few moments at a time. They may get a faint glimmer of faith and the peace that seems to be within reach. Then all the old doubts spring up again with tenfold power.

"Look at your heart," they say. "See how cold it is, how indifferent. How can you for a moment believe that God can love such a poor, unworthy creature as you?" It all sounds so reasonable that they are plunged into darkness again.

The trouble arises from a lack of faith. It seems repetitous to say it, but the stability in our spiritual life is *always* directly related to our faith.

This is a spiritual law that can neither be neglected nor evaded. It is not an arbitrary law. We cannot hope that it would be repealed in our special case. It is inherent in the very nature of things. It is, quite simply, unalterable. Equally unalterable is its converse. If it is to be done to us according to our faith, so will it also be done to us according to our doubt.

The root of our wavering experience is not our sins. It is simply and only our doubts. Doubts create an impassable gulf between our soul and the Lord, just as they do between us and our earthly friends. No amount of fervor or earnestness can bridge this gulf in either case.

James said, concerning the man who wavers, "Let not that man think that he shall receive any thing of the Lord" (James 1:7). This is not because God is angry and sends His displeasure on the man who doubts. It is simply impossible for doubt and confidence to exist together, whether in earthly relationships or heavenly.

"And to whom sware he that they should not enter into his rest, but to them that believed not? So we see they could not enter in because of unbelief" (Hebrews 3:18-19). It was not that God would not allow them to enter in as a punishment for their unbelief. They simply *could* not. It was an impossibility. Faith is the only door into the Kingdom of God, and there is no other. If we will not go in by that door, we cannot get in at all. There is no other way.

God's salvation is not a purchase to be made or wages to be earned. It is not a summit to be climbed or a task to be accomplished. It is simply a gift to be accepted. It can only be accepted by faith.

Faith is a necessary element in the acceptance of any gift, whether earthly or heavenly. My friends may put their gifts upon my table or even place them in my lap. But unless I believe in their

186

friendliness enough to accept these gifts, they can never become mine.

Unscriptural Additions

Jesus simply announced the nature of things when He declared, "According to your faith be it unto you" (Matthew 9:29). The sooner we realize this, the better our faith lives will be. All our wavering comes from the fact that we do not believe in this law. We acknowledge that it is in the Bible, but we think it cannot really mean what it says. We feel that there must be some additions made to it.

For example, we suppose that "according to our fervency it shall be unto us," or "according to our begging," or "according to our worthiness." Furthermore, we are inclined to think that these additions of ours are, if anything, the most important part of the whole matter. Consequently, our attention is mostly directed to getting these matters settled. We watch our own feelings and search into our own worthiness or unworthiness very diligently. We overlook the fundamental principle of faith, without which nothing can ever be done.

Our feelings are the most variable things in the universe. Our sense of worthiness or unworthiness changes with our changing moods. Therefore, our faith cannot help but waver. We make the faithfulness of God and the truth of His Word depend upon the state of our feelings.

If any of our friends would doubt us like this,

we would be wounded and indignant beyond measure. No feeling of unworthiness on their part could excuse them in our eyes for such a wavering of their confidence in us. We would far rather our friends even sin against us than doubt us.

No form of sinfulness ever hindered the Lord Jesus from doing His mighty works on the earth. The only thing that hindered Him was unbelief. Among His own neighbors and friends, where naturally He would have liked to perform some of His miracles, we are told that, "He did not many mighty works there because of their unbelief" (Matthew 13:58). It was not that He would not, but simply that He could not. And He cannot in our case, anymore than in theirs.

Some may still think that the man whose faith wavers can receive something from the Lord if only he is fervent and earnest enough. That means that you do not believe that God understands the laws of His Kingdom as well as you do. You believe it is safer to follow your own ideas rather than His Word.

You must know that your doubts have brought you nothing but darkness and misery in the past. Recall the times of halting, stumbling, and discomfort in your religious life. Ask yourself honestly whether the cause of it all has been your wavering faith.

How To Stop Wavering

If you believe one day that God loves you and is

favorable to you, and the next day you doubt His love and fear He is angry with you, you will waver in your experience from joy to misery. Only a steadfast faith in His love and care could give you an unwavering experience.

The question for all whose faith wavers is how to put an end to their wavering forever. The answer is to *give it up*. Your wavering is caused by your doubting and nothing else. Give up your doubting, and your wavering will stop. Keep on with your doubting, and your wavering will continue. The whole matter is as simple as that. The choice is in your own hands.

You may think this is an extreme statement. Maybe you never realized that you could give up doubting. But I assure you that you can. You can simply refuse to doubt. You can shut the door against every suggestion of doubt that comes. By faith you can declare exactly the opposite.

Your doubt says, "God does not forgive my sins." Your faith must say, "He does forgive me; He says He does, and I choose to believe Him. I am His forgiven child." You must assert this steadfastly until all your doubts vanish.

You have no right to say that you are of such a doubting nature that you cannot help doubting. That would be like saying that you are of such a thieving nature that you cannot help stealing. One is as easily controlled as the other. You must give up your doubt just as you would give up your theft. You must treat the temptation to doubt exactly as a drunkard must treat the temptation to drink. You must take a pledge against it.

The process that is the most effective is to lay our doubts, just as our other sins, upon God's altar and make a total surrender of them. We must give up all doubt and consecrate our power of believing to Him. Then we can trust Him to keep us trusting.

Our faith in His Word should be as important as our obedience to His will. We must be as loyal to our heavenly Friend as we are to our earthly friends. Finally, we must refuse any question or doubt concerning His love or His faithfulness. There can be no wavering in our absolute faith in His Word.

Of course, temptations to waver will come. It sometimes looks impossible that the Lord can love such disagreeable, unworthy beings as we feel that we are. We must turn a deaf ear to these insinuations against the love of God just as we would to insinuations against the love of our dearest friend.

The fight to do this may sometimes be very severe, and may even at times seem almost unendurable. But our shout of faith declares, "Though he slay me, yet will I trust in him" (Job 13:15). Our steadfast trust in Him guarantees us a glorious victory.

When we look at our many shortcomings, we may think that a truly humble soul should waver in faith. It may seem to be a righteous thing to question whether the salvation of the Lord Jesus can be meant for us. But if we understand what the salvation of the Lord Jesus Christ is, we will recognize that these questions are only a temptation to sin. Lift up the shield of faith persistently against them. "Above all, taking the shield of faith, wherewith ye shall be able to quench all the fiery darts of the wicked" (Ephesians 6:16).

Perfect Confidence In God

The Spirit of God could never suggest a doubt of the love of God. All doubts are from an evil source, and they must always be treated as the suggestions of an enemy.

We cannot prevent the suggestions of doubt making themselves heard in our hearts, anymore than we can prevent our ears from hearing the curses of wicked men in the streets. But just as we can refuse to agree with the curses of these men, we can refuse to pay attention to these suggestions of doubt. In the case of the oaths, however, we know without any question that it would be wicked to join in with them. In the case of the doubts, we have a lurking feeling that doubts may have something pious in them and ought to be encouraged. I believe one is as displeasing to God as the other.

The most practical way of giving up doubt is to meet each doubt with a flat denial. Then counter it with an emphatic assertion of faith. For instance, suppose the doubt arises as to whether God can love anyone so sinful and unfaithful as you feel yourself to be. Immediately affirm in your own heart, and if possible aloud to someone, that God *does* love you. He says He does, and His Word is worth a million times more trust than any of your feelings. It does not matter how well founded those feelings may seem to you. If you cannot find anyone to say this to, then write it in a letter. Or say it aloud to yourself and to God. Be very definite about it.

If you had a beginning of confidence, if you have ever laid hold of any promise or declaration of the Lord, then hold on steadfastly to that promise or declaration without wavering. There can be no middle ground. If it was true once, it is true still, for God is unchangeable.

The only thing that can deprive you of God's best is your unbelief. While you believe, you have it. "What things soever ye desire, when ye pray, believe that ye receive them, and ye shall have them" (Mark 11:24).

Let nothing shake your faith. If sin overtakes you, do not let it make you doubt. Immediately upon the discovery of any sin, take 1 John 1:9 and act on it. "If we confess our sins, he is faithful and just to forgive us our sins, and to cleanse us from all unrighteousness." Then believe that God does forgive you, as He promised, and does again cleanse you from all unrighteousness.

No sin, however grievous, can separate us from God for one moment after it has been treated in this way. To allow sin to cause your faith to waver is only to add a new sin to the one already committed. Return at once and let your faith hold steadfastly to His Word.

Believe it, not because you feel it or see it, but because He says it. Believe it, even when it seems to you that you are believing a lie. Believe it actively and steadfastly, through dark and through light, through ups and downs, through times of comfort and times of despair. If you do, your wavering experience will end.

"Therefore, my beloved brethren, be ye steadfast, unmoveable, always abounding in the work of the Lord, forasmuch as ye know that your labour is not in vain in the Lord" (2 Corinthians 15:58). To be unmoveable in one's faith is the opposite of wavering.

In the Forty-sixth Psalm we can see what it means. The earth may be removed, and the mountains may be carried into the midst of the sea, and our whole universe may seem to be in ruins. But while we trust in the Lord, we shall not be moved.

The man who wavers in his faith is upset by the smallest troubles. The man who is steadfast in his faith can look on calmly at the ruin of all his universe.

To be immoveable in one's Christian life is a blessing to be strongly desired. It may be ours, if we will only hold the beginning of our confidence steadfast to the end.

Chapter 13

THE PROBLEM OF DISCOURAGEMENT

"The soul of the people was much discouraged because of the way"—Numbers 21:4.

The Church abounds in people who are "discouraged because of the way." Either inwardly or outwardly, and often both, things look all wrong. There seems to be no hope of escape. Christians' souls faint within them, and their religious lives are full of discomfort and misery.

There is nothing that so paralyzes effort as discouragement. Nothing more continually and successfully invites defeat. The secret of failure or success in any matter lies far more in the soul's attitude than in any other cause. It is a law of our being that the inward man causes far more conflict than anything the outward man does or possesses.

Nowhere is this more true than in the spiritual life. The Bible declares from beginning to end that faith is the law of the spiritual life; and that according to our faith, it always will be done for us. Faith and discouragement cannot exist together. Therefore, it is obvious that discouragement is an absolute barrier to faith. Where discouragement rules, the converse to the law of faith must rule also. It will be done to us not according to our faith, but according to our discouragement.

Just as courage is faith in good, so discouragement is faith in evil. While courage opens the door to good, discouragement opens it to evil.

The Source Of Discouragement

Once upon a time, Satan desired to entrap a devoted Christian worker and called a council of his helpers to decide the best way of doing it. After the case was explained, an imp offered himself to do the work.

"How will you do it?" asked Satan.

"Oh," replied the imp, "I will paint for him the delights and pleasures of a life of sin in such glowing colors that he will be eager to enter into it."

"That will not do," said Satan, shaking his head. "The man has tried sin, and he knows better. He knows it leads to misery and ruin, and he will not listen to you."

Then another imp offered himself, and again Satan asked, "What will you do to win the man over?"

"I will show him the trials and the self-denials of a righteous life, and he will be eager to escape from them."

"Ah, that will not do either," said Satan, "for he

has tried righteousness, and he knows that its paths are paths of peace and happiness."

Then a third imp came up and declared that he was sure he could win the man over.

"Why, what will you do," asked Satan, "that you are so sure?"

"I will discourage his soul," replied the imp triumphantly.

"That will do, that will do!" exclaimed Satan. "You will be successful. Go and bring back your victim."

There is an old Quaker saying, "All discouragement is from the devil." I believe it states a far deeper truth than we fully understand. Discouragement cannot have its source in God. The life of the Lord Jesus Christ is a life of faith, good cheer, courage, and hope.

"Be discouraged," says our lower nature, "for the world is a place of temptation and sin."

"Be of good cheer," says Christ, "for I have overcome the world." There cannot possibly be any room for discouragement in a world which Christ has overcome.

In temporal things, perhaps, we have learned that discouragement is foolish and even wrong. But when it comes to spiritual things, we are tempted to reverse our opinion and make it commendable. We even succeed in persuading ourselves that to be discouraged is a very humble state of mind.

The causes for our discouragement often seem

so legitimate. The first and perhaps most common of these causes is our own weaknesses. It is right for us to be discouraged, we think, because we know that we are such poor, miserable, good-for-nothing creatures. It would be presumption, in the face of such incapacity, to be anything but discouraged.

No Excuses For God's People

Moses had to overcome deep discouragement. The Lord called him to lead the children of Israel out of the land of Egypt. Moses looked at his own natural infirmities and weaknesses and tried to excuse himself. "I am not eloquent. . .but I am slow of speech, and of a slow tongue. . . .They will not believe me nor hearken unto my voice" (Exodus 4:10;1).

Naturally, one would think that Moses had plenty of reasons to be discouraged. We may be attacked in the same way that he was. We distrust our own eloquence or our own power to convince those to whom we are sent, so we shrink from the work which the Lord may be calling us to do.

But notice how the Lord answered Moses, for He answers us in the same way. God did not try to convince Moses that he really was eloquent or that his tongue was not slow of speech. He passed all this by, because it did not matter. There could not possibly be any reason for discouragement, even if Moses did have all the infirmities of speech that he had complained about.

"And the Lord said unto him, Who hath made man's mouth? or who maketh the dumb, or deaf, or the seeing, or the blind? have not I, the Lord? Now therefore go, and I will be with thy mouth, and teach thee what thou shalt say" (Exodus 4:11-12).

The word of the Lord came to Jeremiah telling him that God had ordained him to be a prophet to the nations. Jeremiah felt himself to be entirely unequal to such a work and said, "Ah, Lord God! behold, I cannot speak, for I am a child." But the Lord answered, "Say not, I am a child: for thou shalt go to all that I shall send thee, and whatsoever I command thee thou shalt speak. Be not afraid of their faces: for I am with thee to deliver thee, saith the Lord" (Jeremiah 1:6-8).

The Story of Gideon gives us another illustration. The Lord called him to lead the deliverance of His people from the oppression of the Midianites. He said to Gideon, "Go in this thy might, and thou shalt save Israel, from the hands of the Midianites: have I not sent thee?" (Judges 6:14).

This should have been enough for Gideon. But he was a poor, unknown man. He had no apparent qualifications for such a great mission. Looking at himself and his own deficiencies, he naturally became discouraged and said, "Wherewith shall I save Israel? behold my family is poor in Manasseh, and I am the least in my father's house" (Judges 6:15). Other men who had power and influence might perhaps accomplish this great work, but not one so poor and insignificant as Gideon.

How familiar this conversation must sound to the victims of discouragement and how sensible and reasonable it seems. But what did the Lord think of it? "And the Lord said unto him, Surely I will be with thee, and thou shalt smite the Midianites as one man" (Judges 6:16).

The Promise Of His Presence

All that was given was the promise, "Surely I will be with thee." Not one word of encouragement did the Lord give Gideon concerning his capacity or fitness for the work required. He merely made the promise that is sufficient for all possible needs, "I will be with thee."

To all words of discouragement in the Bible, this is the invariable answer: "I will be with thee." It is an answer that removed all reason for argument or any further discouragement. "I, your Creator and Redeemer, I your strength and wisdom, I your omnipresent and omniscient God, I will be with you and will protect you through everything. No enemy will hurt you; no accusations of man will disturb you. My presence will be your safety and defense."

One would think that in the face of such assertions as these, not even the most faint-hearted among us could find any excuse for discouragement. But discouragement comes in many subtle forms. Our spiritual enemies attack us in many disguises.

We are often our own worst enemy. Other people can be cheerful and courageous, we think. But we should be discouraged. We see how foolish, how helpless, how unfit to grapple with any enemies we are.

There would indeed be ample cause for discouragement if we had to fight our battles ourselves. We would be right in thinking we could not do it. But if the Lord is to fight them for us, it puts an entirely different light on the matter. Our lack of ability to fight becomes an advantage instead of a disadvantage. We can only be strong in Him when we are weak in ourselves. Our weakness, therefore, is our greatest strength.

A Lesson From Israel

The children of Israel can give us a lesson here. The Lord had delivered them out of Egypt and had brought them to the borders of the Promised Land. Moses urged them to go up and possess it. "Behold, the Lord thy God hath set the land before thee: go up and possess it, as the Lord God of thy fathers hath said unto thee; fear not, neither be discouraged" (Deuteronomy 1:21).

But the circumstances were so discouraging. They felt so helpless that they could not believe God would actually do all He had said. They murmured in their tents. They even declared that it must be because the Lord hated them that He had brought them out of Egypt in order to deliver them into the hands of their enemies.

And they said, "Whither shall we go up? Our brethren have discouraged our heart, saying, the people is greater and taller than we; the cities are great and walled up to heaven; and moreover we have seen the sons of the Anakims there" (Deuteronomy 1:28).

When we read the report of the spies, we cannot be surprised at their discouragement. We can even understand their feelings that courage under such circumstances would be only foolhardiness.

"The land through which we have gone to search it," the spies declared, "is a land that eateth up the inhabitants thereof; and all the people that we saw in it are men of a great stature. And there we saw the giants, the sons of Anak, which comes of the giants: and we were in our own sight as grasshoppers, and so we were in their sight" (Numbers 14:32-33).

Nothing could have seemed more humble than for them to look upon themselves as poor, good-for-nothing grasshoppers. True humility would seem to teach that it would be the height of presumption for grasshoppers to try to conquer giants. We often feel that we also are merely grasshoppers in face of the giants of temptation and trouble that assail us. We think that we are justified in being discouraged. But the question is not whether we are grasshoppers, but whether God is able to fight for us. It is not we who have to fight these giants, but it is God's battle.

In vain, Moses reminded the Israelites of this. He assured them that they had no need to be afraid of the sons of the Anakims, for the Lord their God would fight for them. He reminded them of past deliverances. He even asked them if they did not remember how "in the wilderness. . .the Lord thy God bare thee, as a man doth bear his son, in all the way that ye went" (Deuteronomy 1:31).

But they were still too discouraged to believe. And the result was that not one of that generation was allowed to see the Promised Land, except Caleb and Joshua. Only these two had steadfastly believed that God could and would lead them in. These are the results of giving in to discouragement, and this is the reward of a steadfast faith.

Trusting God Boldly

The apostle Paul commented on this story in his letter to the Hebrews. "And to whom sware he that they should not enter into his rest, but to them that believed not? So we see that they could not enter in because of unbelief" (Hebrews 3:18-19).

Is there a parallel here to our own circumstances? Do we look at our weakness instead of looking at the Lord's strength? Have we sometimes become so discouraged that we sink into spiritual anguish? Do we reach the point where we cannot even listen to the Lord's own declaration that He will fight for us and give us the victory?

Our souls long to enter into the rest the Lord has promised. But fierce giants seem to stand in our path. We are afraid to believe. So we too, like the Israelites, cannot enter in because of unbelief.

How different it would be if we had enough faith to say with the psalmist, "Though an host should encamp against me, my heart shall not fear: though war should rise against me, in this will I be confident. . . .For in the time of trouble he shall hide me in his pavilion: in the secret of his tabernacle shall he hide me; he shall set me up upon a rock" (Psalm 27:3,5). How joyfully and triumphantly would we be able to enter into rest, if this was our language.

Another very subtle cause for discouragement is the fear of man. There seems to exist a group of people called "they" who rule our lives with an iron hand of control. What will "they" say? What will "they" think? These are among the most frequent questions that harass the timid soul when it seeks to work for the Lord. At every turn, this all-powerful and forever-present "they" stands in our way to discourage us and make us afraid.

This form of discouragement often comes under the disguise of polite consideration for the opinions of others. But it is especially dangerous because it exalts "they" into the place of God and esteems "their" opinions above His promises. The only remedy here, as in all other forms of discouragement, is simply to repeat the fact that God is with us.

"Be not afraid of their faces: for I am with thee to deliver thee, saith the Lord" (Jeremiah 1:8). "For he hath said, I will never leave thee, nor forsake thee. So that we may boldly say, The Lord is my helper, and I will not fear what man shall do unto me" (Hebrews 13:5-6). How can any heart, however timid, dare to indulge in discouragement in the face of such assertions as these?

There is one sort of discouragement that is very common. This is the discouragement that arises from our own failures. It was from this sort of discouragement that the children of Israel suffered after their defeat at Ai. They had "committed a trespass in the accursed thing" (Joshua 7:1). Therefore, they could not stand before their enemies. So great was their discouragement that it is said, "Wherefore the hearts of the people melted, and became as water. And Joshua rent his clothes, and fell to the earth upon his face before the ark of the Lord until the eventide, he and all the elders of Israel, and put dust upon their heads" (Joshua 7:5-6).

When God's own people turn their backs before their enemies, one might think they should lie on their faces and put dust on their heads because they have brought dishonor upon His great name. Discouragement and despair seem to be the only proper action after such failures.

But the Lord thought otherwise, for He said to Joshua, "Get thee up; wherefore liest thou upon thy face?" (Joshua 7:10). The proper thing to do after a failure is not to give in to utter discouragement, humble as this may appear. Rather, face the evil at once and get rid of it. Then consecrate yourself again to the Lord, afresh and immediately. "Up, sanctify yourselves" is always God's command. "Lie down and be discouraged" is always our temptation.

The Holy Spirit's Role

But should a sense of sin produced by the conviction of the Holy Spirit cause discouragement? If I see myself to be a sinner, how can I help being discouraged? The Holy Spirit does not convict us of sin in order to discourage us, but to encourage us. His work is to show us our sin, not that we may lie down in despair under its power, but that we may get rid of it.

A good mother points out the faults of her children for the purpose of helping them correct those faults. The convictions of the Holy Spirit are truly one of our greatest blessings. They do not mean that we are to give up in discouragement. Rather, we are to be encouraged to believe that deliverance is coming.

The good housewife does not look for stains on her tablecloth in order that she may throw it aside as no longer fit for use. Instead, she cleans it so that she may use it again. If she is a good laundress, she will not be discouraged by the worst of stains.

God says to us, "Though your sins be as scarlet,

they shall be as white as snow" (Isaiah 1:18). Pure unbelief on our part allows us to be discouraged at even the worst of our failures. God's cleansing must be at least as effective as the washing of any human laundress.

Fenelon says concerning this, "It is of great importance to guard against discouragement on account of our faults. Discouragement is not a fruit of humility, but of pride, and nothing can be worse. It springs from a secret love of our own excellence. We are hurt at feeling what we are. If we become discouraged we are the more enfeebled, and from our reflections on our own imperfections, a chagrin arises that is often worse than the imperfection itself. Poor nature longs from self love to behold itself perfect. It is vexed that it is not so. It is impatient, haughty, and out of temper with itself and with everybody else. Sad state, as though the work of God could be accomplished by our ill-humour. As though the peace of God could be attained by our interior restlessness."

The Importance Of Speaking Right

Discouragement, from whatever source it may come, produces many sad results. One of its very worst is that it leads people to murmur and to speak against God. When the children of Israel were discouraged because of the way, we are told that they "spake against God" and asked all sort of God-dishonoring questions. (See Numbers 21:4-5.)

The rebelling and murmuring thoughts that sometimes beset us always begin in discouragement. Discouragement is a "speaking against God." It implies some sort of a failure on His part to give us what His promises have led us to expect of Him.

The psalmist recognized this. He says, concerning the questions asked in the days of their wilderness wandering, "Yea, they spake against God; they said, Can God furnish a table in the wilderness?" (Psalm 78:19).

It appears that our questions concerning God's willingness to help us are more than humble inquiries. They may seem reasonable to us and even humble. In reality, we are "speaking against God." The questions are displeasing to Him, because they reveal the sad fact that we "believe not in God, and trusted not in his salvation" (Psalm 78:22).

Another grievous quality in discouragement is that it is contagious. The spies sent out by Moses brought up a bad report of the Promised Land and told of the giants there. They discouraged the hearts of their brethren so that the people lifted up their voices and cried. They refused to go into the land which the Lord had given them and which they had started out to possess. (See Numbers 13:27-33; 14:1-3.)

The bad report that many Christians bring of their failures and their disappointments is the subject of many discouraging conversations. The hearts of many young Christians are far too often discouraged by their older brethren. The older Christians have little idea of the harm they are doing by their sorrowful accounts of the trials of the Christian experience.

The Lord felt that it was important that no one should discourage another's heart. When Moses gave God's law to the Israelites concerning their methods of warfare, he said, "And the officers shall speak further unto the people, and they shall say, What man is there that is fearful and fainthearted? let him go and return unto his house, lest his brethren's heart faint as well as his heart" (Deuteronomy 20:8).

Discouraged people should keep their discouragement to themselves. They should hide their feelings in the privacy of their own heart, lest they discourage the hearts of their brethren. We know that courage is contagious. One brave soul in a moment of danger can save a crowd from a panic. But we often fail to remember that the opposite of this is also true. One faint-hearted man or woman can infect a whole crowd with fear.

Filled With Joy And Courage

If the Body of Christ would remove all the hymns of discouragement from its hymn books and would allow only hymns of good cheer to be sung, the faith of Christians would be strengthened.

"Be of good cheer," is the command of the Lord for His disciples, "I have overcome the world.

(John 16:33). Therefore, there is nothing left for us to be discouraged about. If we understood what it means that Christ has overcome the world, we would be shocked at the idea of any one of His followers ever becoming discouraged again.

If you had been an Israelite in the days of Joshua, would you have been one of the spies who brought back an evil report of the land? Would you have discouraged the hearts of their brethren and brought upon them the dreary, forty years of wilderness wandering? Or would you have been like Caleb and Joshua, who "stilled the people before Moses, and said, Let us go up at once, and possess it; for we are well able to overcome it" (Numbers 13:30)?

In the divine review of this episode, Moses spoke of Caleb as one who had wholly followed the Lord" (Numbers 32:12). This was because Caleb had given the Israelites a good report of their land. When his fellow spies had made the heart of the people to melt by their evil report, Caleb had encouraged them to go up and possess the land.

Many truly devoted Christians fail in the essential point of wholly following the Lord. The principle mission of their lives appears to be discouraging the hearts of their brethren by the sorrowful reports they bring of the difficulties of the Christian life.

How different it would be if discouragement was looked upon in its true light as a "speaking against God." What a blessing it would be if only encouraging words were heard among Christians. How many times would the children of Israel have failed in conquering their enemies had there been no men of faith among them to encourage and cheer them. On the other hand, who can tell how many spiritual defeats and disasters that discouraging words may have brought about in your own life and in the lives of those around you?

One of Isaiah's prophecies begins with, "Comfort ye, comfort ye my people, saith your God." Isaiah gives us a wonderful description of God as the reason for comfort. Then he sets forth what God's people ought to be and says, "They helped every one his neighbour; and every one said to his brother, Be of good courage. So the carpenter encouraged the goldsmith, and he that smootheth with the hammer him that smote the anvil" (Isaiah 41:6-7). Shall we follow their example and encourage one another?

Like so many other wrong spiritual habits, we must give discouragment up in order to get rid of it. It is never worthwhile to argue against discouragment. There is only one argument that can meet it, and that is the argument of God.

David was in the midst of the most discouraging moments of his life. He found his city burned and his wives stolen. He and the men with him had wept until they had no more power to weep. When his men, exasperated at their misfortunes, spoke of stoning him, we are told, "But David encouraged himself in the Lord his God" (1 Samuel 30:6).

The result was a magnificent victory. All that they had lost was more than restored to them. This will always be the result of a courageous faith, because faith lays hold of the omnipotence of God.

The psalmist asks himself this question, "Why art thou cast down, O my soul? and why art thou disquieted in me?" And each time he answers himself with the argument of God. "Hope thou in God: for I shall yet praise him, who is the health of my countenance, and my God" (Psalm 42:11). He does not analyze his discouragement or try to argue it away. Rather, he turns at once to the Lord and by faith begins to praise Him.

This is the only way to overcome. Discouragement flies where faith appears. The opposite is also true—faith flies when discouragement appears. We must choose between them, for they will not mix.

Chapter 14

THE SHOUT OF FAITH

"And when ye hear the sound of the trumpet, all the people shall shout with a great shout; and the wall of the city shall fall down flat, and the people shall ascend up every man straight before him"—Joshua 6:5.

The shout of steadfast faith contrasts sharply with the moans of a wavering faith and the wails of discouraged hearts. In the history of the children of Israel, there were many occasions when they indulged in these moanings and wailings. It always led to their sad undoing.

On one occasion, however, they gave a magnificent shout of steadfast faith that brought them a glorious victory. Among the many secrets of the Lord that are discovered by the soul in its spiritual growth, none is more valuable than the secret of the shout of faith.

God Makes A Promise

The Israelites had just crossed the river Jordan

and were about to take possession of the Promised Land. God said to Joshua just before they crossed, "Now therefore arise, go over this Jordan, thou, and all this people, unto the land which I do give to them, even to the children of Israel. Every place that the sole of your foot shall tread upon, that have I given unto you, as I said unto Moses" (Joshua 1:2-3).

With this promise, they crossed the river and entered into the land, no doubt expecting to get immediate possession. But they were facing one of those "cities great and walled up to heaven" that had discouraged the heart of the spies forty years before. (See Deuteronomy 1:28.) They had good reason to be appalled at the sight of it. To the eye of their senses, there seemed no possibility that they could ever conquer Jericho. They had no engines of warfare with which to attack it. One can easily imagine the despair that must have seized them when they found themselves confronted with the walls and fortresses of the city.

But the Lord said to Joshua, "See, I have given into thine hand Jericho, and the king thereof, and the mighty men of valour" (Joshua 6:2). He had not said, "I will give," but, "I have given." It belonged to them already. Now they were called upon to take possession of it. It was as if a king bestowed an estate upon his ambassador who was away in a foreign land. The ambassador must come back to take possession of it.

The great question was: How? It looked impossible. But the Lord had a plan. After a few directions concerning the order of their march and the blowing of their trumpets, He closed with these strange words, "And it shall come to pass, that when they make a long blast with the ram's horn, and when ye hear the sound of the trumpet, all the people shall shout with a great shout; and the wall of the city shall fall down flat, and the people shall ascend up every man straight before him" (Joshua 6:5).

Strange words but true, for it came to pass just as the Lord had said. On the seventh day when the priests blew the trumpets, Joshua said to the people, "Shout; for the Lord hath given you the city. . . .And it came to pass, when the people heard the sound of the trumpet, and the people shouted with a great shout, that the wall fell down flat, so that the people went up into the city, every man straight before him, and they took the city" (Joshua 6:16,20).

No one can suppose that this shout caused the walls to fall. Yet, the secret of their victory lay in this shout. It was the shout of a faith which dared, on the authority of God's Word alone, to claim a promised victory. They shouted even though there were no signs of this victory being accomplished. And according to their faith God gave them a miracle. When they shouted, He made the walls fall.

God declared that He had given them the city, and faith considered this to be true. Unbelief might say, "It would be better not to shout until the walls actually do fall. Then if we fail and the men of Jericho triumph, we will not bring dishonor on the name of our God."

But faith laughed at all such timid considerations and confidently rested on God's Word. It gave a shout of victory, while to the physical eye that victory seemed impossible. Centuries later, the Holy Spirit records this triumph of faith in Hebrews: "By faith the walls of Jericho fell down, after they were compassed about seven days" (Hebrews 11:30).

Jehoshaphat Under Attack

Jehoshaphat gives us another example of this shout of faith. He was told that a great multitude was coming up against him. He realized that he and his people had no chance against them, but he did not waste his time and energy by preparing for war or in arranging plans for a battle. Instead, he at once "set himself to seek the Lord" (2 Chronicles 20:3).

Jehoshaphat stood in the congregation of the people and said, "O Lord God of our fathers, art not thou God in heaven? and rulest not thou over all the kingdoms of the heathen? and in thine hand is there not power and might, so that none is able to withstand thee? Art not thou our God, who didst drive out the inhabitants of this land before thy people Israel, and gavest it to the seed of Abraham thy friend for ever?. . .And now, behold, the children of Ammon and Moab and mount Seir. . .come to cast us out of thy possession, which thou hast given us to inherit. O our God, wilt thou not judge them? for we have no might against this great company that cometh against us; neither know we what to do: but our eyes are upon thee" (2 Chronicles 20:6-7,10-11).

The Lord answered through the mouth of His prophet, "Thus saith the Lord unto you, Be not afraid nor dismayed by reason of this great multitude; for the battle is not yours, but God's. . . .Ye shall not need to fight in this battle: set yourselves, stand ye still, and see the salvation of the Lord with you, O Judah and Jerusalem: fear not, nor be dismayed; to morrow go out against them: for the Lord will be with you" (2 Chronicles 20:15,17).

Jehoshaphat and the children of Israel believed the Word of the Lord and began at once to praise Him for the victory that they were sure was coming. The next morning they rose early and went out to meet their enemy. Jehoshaphat, instead of exhorting them to be brave in battle, simply called upon them to have a courageous faith. "Hear me, O Judah, and ye inhabitants of Jerusalem; Believe in the Lord your God, so shall ye be established; believe his prophets, so shall ye prosper" (2 Chronicles 20:20).

Jehoshaphat then appointed singers to go out before the army to sing praises as they went forward to meet the enemy. When they began to sing and praise, the Lord set up an ambush so that the enemy forces were confused, and they began to kill one another. When the children of Israel came to a watchtower in the wilderness, they could see the great multitude that had come up against them. What they saw was "dead bodies fallen to the earth, and none escaped" (2 Chronicles 20:24).

By this wonderful method of warfare, they were made even more than conquerors. It took them three days to gather the spoil that their vanquished foes left behind. (See 2 Chronicles 20:25.)

David And Goliath

David's fight with Goliath is another account of victory. To the physical eye, David had no chance of conquering the mighty Giant who had defied the armies of Israel. But David, looking with the eye of faith, knew that the unseen divine forces were fighting on his side.

Saul said to him, "Thou art not able to go against this Philistine to fight with him: for thou art but a youth, and he a man of war from his youth" (1 Samuel 17:33). But David stood firm in his faith. After recounting some of his past deliverances, he said calmly, "The Lord that delivered me out of the paw of the lion, and out of the paw of the bear, he will deliver me out of the hand of this Philistine." Saul, partly convinced by this strong faith, said, "Go, and the Lord be with thee" (1 Samuel 17:37).

Saul could not, however, give up all trust in his own armor. He gave David a helmet of brass, a coat of mail, and his own powerful sword. But David found that he would not be able to fight in this sort of armor. He took it off and took instead the simple weapons that the Lord had blessed before—his staff, his sling, and five smooth stones from the brook. Thus equipped, he drew near to the Giant.

When the Giant saw the youth who had come to fight him, he laughed at David. "Come to me, and I will give thy flesh unto the fowls of the air, and the beasts of the field" (1 Samuel 17:44). To the eye of sense, it certainly looked as though this would be the end of such an apparently unequal battle.

But David's faith triumphed, and he shouted a shout of victory before the battle had even begun. "Thou comest to me with a sword, and with a spear, and with a shield: but I come to thee in the name of the Lord of hosts, the God of the armies of Israel, whom thou hast defied. This day will the Lord deliver thee into mine hands and I will smite thee, and take thy head from thee. . .that all the earth may know that there is a God in Israel. And all this assembly shall know that the Lord saveth not with sword and spear: for the battle is the Lord's, and he will give you into our hands" (1 Samuel 17:45-47).

In the face of such faith as this, what could even a Giant do? Every word of David's triumphant shout of victory was fulfilled. The mighty enemy was delivered into the hands of the boy he had disdained. Nothing can withstand the triumphant faith that links itself to omnipotence. "This is the victory that overcometh the world, even our faith" (1 John 5:4).

Secrets of Successful Warfare

The secret of all successful warfare lies in this shout of faith. It is an incomprehensible secret to those who do not know the unseen divine power that waits on the demands of faith. The secret must always seem, to those who do not understand it, the height of foolishness.

We are all called to be good soldiers of Jesus Christ and to fight the good fight of faith. We face worse enemies than those which attacked the Israelites. Our enemies are within us. The giant that defies us is the strength of our temptations and the powerlessness of our own strength to resist.

It is a hard and often discouraging fight. Many of God's children are weighed down under a sense of apparently hopeless failure. They have sinned, repented, prayed, resolved, and then sinned and repented again. This has gone on for so long that they can see no hope of victory and are ready to despair. They hate sin, and they love righteousness. They long for victory.

In the language of the apostle Paul, they find a law in their flesh warring against the law of their mind. It brings them into captivity to the law of sin that is in their members. (See Romans 7:18-21.) They know they should conquer, but they do not know how. If they discover the secret of this shout of faith, they will know how. It is absolutely certain that it never fails to bring victory.

In John 16:33, our Lord reveals the reason for this triumphant shout of faith. "Be of good cheer," He says, "for I have overcome the world." Not "I will overcome," but "I have overcome." It is already done; and nothing remains but for us to enter into the power of it.

Joshua did not say to the people "Shout, for the Lord *will* give you the city." Rather, he said, "Shout, for he *hath* given it." It must have taken all Joshua's faith for him to make such a statement. The walls of the city were standing as massive and as impregnable as ever. But God was a reality to Joshua. He was not afraid to proclaim the victory that had been promised, even before it was accomplished.

There is a great difference between saying, "The Lord will give" and "The Lord hath given." A victory, promised in the future, may be hindered or prevented by a thousand difficulties. But a victory already accomplished cannot be denied.

When our Lord assures us that He has already overcome the world, He gives a foundation for a shout of the most triumphant victory. From then on, the forces of sin are a defeated and demoralized foe. If we believe the words of Christ, we can meet our foes without fear. We know that we have been made more than conquerors through Him who loves us.

The secret then lies in this: we must meet sin, not as a foe that has yet to be conquered, but as one that has already been conquered. When Rahab helped the spies to escape from the King of Jericho, she made this confession, "I know that the Lord hath given you the land, and that your terror is fallen upon us, and that all the inhabitants of the land faint because of you" (Joshua 2:9).

Finding Weapons For Warfare

If we were gifted with eyes that could see the unseen kingdom of evil, we would also find that terror and faintness have fallen upon all the forces of that realm. They see in every man and woman of faith a sure and triumphant conqueror. Because we do not know this secret, we meet our spiritual enemies with fear and trembling. This is why we suffer such disastrous defeats.

A Christian who had been fearfully tormented by temptation seemed to struggle against it in vain. She was told the secret of the shout by one who had discovered it. It brought conviction at once, and then she went forth to battle with the assurance of an already accomplished victory. Of course, she was victorious.

She said afterward that it was as if she could almost hear the voice of the tempter saying as he crept away, "Alas! it is all up with me now. She has found out the secret. She knows that I am an already conquered foe. I am afraid I shall never be able to overcome her again!"

We are told that, "For this purpose the Son of God was manifested, that he might destroy the works of the devil" (1 John 3:8). "And ye know that he was manifested to take away our sins; and in him is no sin" (1 John 3:5). "Now once in the end of the world hath he appeared to put away sin by the sacrifice of himself" (Hebrews 10:26). We must accept it as a fact, therefore, that sin is for us a conquered foe.

We must consider ourselves to be dead to sin. We need to dare, in spite of temptation, to raise the shout of victory. Then we will surely find, as the Israelites did, that every wall will fall down flat. A pathway will be opened up straight before us to take the city!

Our enemies are giants now just as truly as they were in Israel's day. Cities as great as Jericho, with walls as high, confront us in our heavenly pathway. Like the Israelites of old, we have no human weapons with which to conquer them. Our armor, like theirs, must be the armor of God. Our shield is the same invisible shield of faith that protected them. Our sword must be, as theirs was, the sword of the Spirit which is the Word, the promises, and the declarations of God.

When our faith puts on this armor of God and lays hold of this sword of the Spirit, and we confront our enemy with a shout of undaunted faith, we cannot fail to conquer the mightiest giant or to take the strongest city.

Declaring Unseen Victories

But alas! how different is the usual method of our Christian warfare. Instead of a triumphant shout of victory, we meet our temptations with feeble resolutions or futile arguments. When all else fails we pray desperately, "O Lord, save me! O Lord, deliver me!" If no deliverance comes immediately, the temptation sweeps aside all our arguments and resolutions, and we are grievously defeated. We cry out in our despair that God has failed us. We insist that there is for us no truth in Paul's declaration, that with every temptation there is "a way to escape, that ye may be able to bear it" (1 Corinthians 10:13). This is the usual and the unsuccessful way of meeting temptation, as many of us know from experience.

The walls may look as high and immoveable as ever. We may be cautious and say it is not safe to shout until the victory is actually won. But faith can shout in the midst of the worst stress of temptation, "Jesus saves me; He saves me now!" Such faith will be sure to win a glorious and a speedy victory.

Many of God's children have tried this and have found it to work far beyond even their expectations. Temptations come in upon them like a flood—temptations to irritability, wicked thoughts, bitterness of spirit, or to a thousand other things. They have seen their danger. Their fears and their feelings declared that there was no hope of escape.

But their faith laid hold of the grand fact that Christ has conquered. Fixing their gaze on the unseen power of God's salvation, they give their shout of victory. "The Lord saves! He saves' me now! I am more than a conqueror through Him that loves me!" The result is always a glorious victory.

These declarations of faith often seem untrue at first. The seen reasons for doubt and discouragement seem so real. But the unseen facts are truer than the seen. If faith remains steadfast, the promises never fail. According to our faith, it always must be given to us, sooner or later. When we shout the shout of faith, the Lord always gives the victory of faith.

I once knew a Christian dock worker who had begun this life of faith. He had a naturally violent temper. While doing his daily work among his ungodly companions, he was sorely tempted to give way to rage. He knew it was wrong. He struggled valiantly against it, but it seemed to be all in vain.

Finally, one morning on his way to work, he called in despair at the house of his pastor and told him his difficulties. He explained the suddenness of the temptations that came upon him and the lack of time even to pray for help before he was overcome.

He asked the minister, "Now can you tell me of

any short road to victory; something that I can lay hold of just at the needed moment?"

"Yes," replied the minister. "When the temptation comes, at once lift up your heart to the Lord, and by faith claim the promised victory. Shout the shout of faith, and the temptation will flee before you."

After a little explanation of the glorious fact that sin is an already conquered foe, the dock worker seemed to understand. He went on his way to take his place in the ranks with his fellow workers at the station where they were hauling freight. As usual he was met by taunts and jeers because of his faith. They pushed him out of his rightful place in the line. The temptation to anger was almost overwhelming, but folding his arms, he said inwardly over and over, "Jesus saves me; He saves me now!" At once his heart was filled with peace, and the victory was complete.

Again he was tried. A heavy box was deliberately rolled so that it fell on his foot and badly hurt him. Again he folded his arms and repeated his shout of victory, and at once all was calm. And so the day passed on. Trials and temptations abounded, but his triumphant shout carried him safely through them all. The fiery darts of the enemy were all quenched by the shield of faith he continually lifted up. Evening found him more than conqueror through Him who loved him. Even his fellow workers were forced to admit the reality and the beauty of a faith that could triumph over their aggravating assaults.

The psalmist, after telling of the enemies who were daily trying to defeat him, declared triumphantly, "When I cry unto thee, then shall mine enemies turn back: this I know; for God is for me" (Psalm 56:9).

Do you know what the psalmist knew? Do you know that God is for you, and that He will cause your enemies to turn back? If you do, then go out to meet your temptations, singing a song of triumph.

Meet your very next temptation in this way. At its first approach, begin to give thanks for the victory. Continually claim that you are more than a conqueror through Him that loves you and refuse to be defeated by any foe. Shout the shout of faith with Joshua, Jehoshaphat, David, and Paul. When you shout, the Lord will send ambushes and all your enemies will fall defeated before you.

Chapter 15

THANKSGIVING VERSUS COMPLAINING

"In everything give thanks: for this is the will of God in Christ Jesus concerning you"—1 Thessalonians 5:18.

Thanksgiving and complaining—these words express two contrasting attitudes of God's children regarding His dealings with them. These attitudes are more powerful than we tend to believe. They either further or frustrate His plans of comfort and peace toward us. The soul that gives thanks can find comfort in everything; the soul that complains can find comfort in nothing.

God's command is, "In everything give thanks." The command is emphasized by the declaration, "for this is the will of God in Christ Jesus concerning you." It is a positive command. If we want to obey God, we must give thanks in everything. There is no getting around it.

But a great many Christians have never realized this. Although they may be familiar with the command, they look upon it as a sort of concept of perfection which mere flesh and blood could never be expected to reach. Unconsciously perhaps, they change the wording of the passage and make it say, "be resigned" instead of, "give thanks." They say, "in a few things" instead of, "in everything," and they leave out altogether the words "for this is the will of God in Christ Jesus concerning you."

If brought face to face with the actual wording of the command, these Christians will say, "Oh, but it is an impossible command. If everything came directly from God, one might do it perhaps. But most things come through human sources and often are the result of sin. It would not be possible to give thanks for these." It is true we cannot always give thanks for the things themselves, but we can always give thanks for God's love and care in the things. He may not have ordered them, but He is in them somewhere. He will cause even the most painful to work together for our good.

The apparent causes of the wrong may be full of malice and wickedness, but faith never sees these causes. It sees only the hand of God behind them. They are all under His control. Not one of them can touch us except with His knowledge and permission. The thing that happens cannot perhaps be said to be the will of God. But by the time its effects reach us, it has become God's will for us and must be accepted from His hands.

Turning Trials To Triumphs

The story of Joseph illustrates this. Nothing could have seemed more wicked or more contrary to the will of God than Joseph being sold to the Ishmaelites by his cruel brothers. It would not have seemed possible for Joseph when he was being carried off into slavery in Egypt to give thanks.

And yet, if he had known the end from the beginning, he would have been filled with thanksgiving. Being sold into slavery was the direct doorway to the greatest triumphs and blessings of his life. At the end, Joseph could say to his brothers, "But as for you, ye thought evil against me; but God meant it unto good" (Genesis 50:20). To the physical eye, it was Joseph's wicked brothers who sent him into Egypt; but Joseph, looking with the eye of faith, said, "God did send me."

We can all remember instances in our lives when God caused even the hardest trials to work together for our good. I remember when a trial was brought upon me by another person. I was filled with bitter rebellion and could not see any reason to be thankful in it.

But like Joseph, that very trial provided the richest blessings and the greatest triumphs of my life. In the end, I was filled with thanksgiving for the things that had caused me such bitter rebellion before. If only I had faith enough to give thanks at first, how much sorrow I would have been spared.

Unfortunately, the greatest heights to which most Christians in their short-sightedness seem able to rise is to strive for resignation to things they cannot change. They pray for patience to endure life's difficulties. The result is that thanksgiving is an almost unknown exercise among the children of God. Instead of giving thanks in everything, many of them hardly give thanks in anything.

Christians as a whole are a thankless group. The world considers it very rude for one man to receive benefits from another man and fail to thank him. Why then, is it not just as discourteous to fail to thank God? There are people who would never forget to send a note of thanks for any small gift from a friend. Yet, they have never given God thanks for one of the innumerable benefits He has been showering upon them their entire lives.

A great many not only fail to give thanks, but they do exactly the opposite. They allow themselves to complain and murmur about God's dealings with them. Instead of looking for His goodness, they seem to delight in picking out His shortcomings. They think they show a spirit of discernment in criticizing His laws and His ways.

We are told that "when the people complained, it displeased the Lord" (Numbers 11:1). But we are tempted to think that our complaining, because it is spiritual complaining, cannot displease Him. Since it is a pious sort of complaining, we think that it is a sign of greater zeal on our part. We feel that we have deeper spiritual insight than is possessed by the ordinary Christian.

But complaining is the same whether it is on the temporal or the spiritual level. It always has in it the element of faultfinding. Webster says that to complain means to make a charge or an accusation. It is more than merely disliking the thing that we have to bear. It contains the element of finding fault with the agency that lies behind it.

If we carefully examine the true source of our complaints, we will find they are founded on fault-finding with God. We secretly feel as if He is to blame somehow. Almost unconsciously, we make mental accusations against Him.

Praising The Giver

Thanksgiving always involves praise of the giver. Have you ever noticed how often we are urged in the Bible to praise the Lord? It seemed to be almost the principal part of the worship of the Israelites. "Praise the Lord; for the Lord is good: sing praises unto his name; for it is pleasant" (Psalm 135:3). This is the continual refrain throughout the Bible. There are more commands given and more examples set for the giving of thanks than for doing anything else.

It is very evident from the whole teaching of Scripture that the Lord loves to be thanked and praised just as much as we do. Our failure to thank

Him for His good and perfect gifts wounds His loving heart, just as our hearts are wounded when our loved ones fail to appreciate the benefits we enjoyed giving them. What a joy it is to us to receive thanks from our friends for our gifts. Certainly it is a joy to the Lord also.

Paul exhorts the Ephesian Christians to be "followers of God, as dear children" (Ephesians 5:1). One of the exhortations he gives, in connection with being filled with the Spirit, is this, "Giving thanks always for all things unto God and the Father in the name of our Lord Jesus Christ" (Ephesians 5:20).

"Always for all things" is a very inclusive expression. It is impossible to suppose it can be whittled down to mean only the scanty thanks, which is all that many Christians manage to give. It must mean that there can be nothing in our lives which does not provide a reason for thanksgiving. No matter who or what may be the channel to convey it, everything contains a hidden blessing from God.

Paul tells us that "every creature of God is good, and nothing to be refused, if it be received with thanksgiving" (1 Timothy 4:4). But it is very hard for us to believe things are good when they do not look that way. Often the things God sends into our lives look like curses instead of blessings. Those who cannot see below the surface judge by the outward appearance only. They never see the blessed realities beneath.

God's Medicine

Even when we realize that things come directly from God, we find it very hard to give thanks for things that hurt us. We all know what it is to thank a skillful physician for his treatment of our diseases, even though that treatment may have been very painful. Surely we should give thanks to our divine Physician when He is obliged to give us bitter medicine to cure our spiritual diseases or to perform a painful operation to rid us of something that harms us.

But instead of thanking Him, we complain against Him. We generally do not direct our complaints against the divine Physician Himself who has ordered our medicine. Rather, we argue against the bottle in which He has sent it. This bottle is usually some human being whose unkindness, carelessness, neglect, or cruelty has caused our suffering. This person has actually been only the instrument that God has used for our healing.

Common sense tells us that it would be foolish to complain against the bottles in which the medicine prescribed by our earthly physicians come to us. It is equally foolish to complain about the situations that are meant to teach us the lessons our souls need to learn.

When the children of Israel found themselves wandering in the wilderness, they murmured against Moses and Aaron. They complained that Moses had brought them into the wilderness to kill them with hunger. (See Exodus 16:3.) In reality, their complaining was against God. He is the one who brought them there, not Moses and Aaron. The psalmist, in recounting the story afterward, referred to this murmuring against Moses and Aaron—"Yea, they spake against God" (Psalm 78:19). Divine history takes no account of apparent causes, but goes directly to the true cause behind them.

All complaining is in reality speaking against God, whether we realize it or not. We may think, as the Israelites did, that our problems have come from people. Therefore, we feel free to murmur against the causes which we think brought about our trials.

But God is the great Cause behind all apparent causes. The apparent causes are only the instruments that He uses. When we murmur against these, we are really murmuring against God Himself. These causes are powerless to act, except by God's permission.

When the Lord heard the complaining of His people, "He was wroth" (Psalm 78:21). His anger came up against them "because they believed not in God, and trusted not in his salvation" (Psalm 78:22). All complaints mean just this—that we do not believe in God and do not trust in His salvation.

The Sacrifice Of Thanksgiving

The psalmist says, "I will praise the name of

234

God with a song, and magnify him with thanksgiving. This also shall please the Lord better than an ox or bullock that hath horns and hoofs" (Psalm 69:30-31).

A great many people seem ready and willing to offer up some great sacrifice to the Lord. But they never realize that a little genuine praise and thanksgiving offered to Him would please Him better than all their great sacrifices.

The *sacrifice of thanksgiving* is an act of worship just like any other religious act. The *sacrifice of thanksgiving* was one of the regular sacrifices ordained by God in the book of Leviticus.

"Oh that men would praise the Lord for his goodness, and for his wonderful works to the children of men! And let them sacrifice the sacrifices of thanksgiving, and declare his works with rejoicing" (Psalm 107:21-22). "By him therefore let us offer the sacrifice of praise to God continually, that is, the fruit of our lips giving thanks to his name" (Hebrews 13:15).

It is such an easy thing to offer the sacrifice of thanksgiving that one would suppose everybody would want to do it. But somehow, the opposite seems to be true. If the prayers of Christians were recorded for a day, we would find that like the ten lepers who had been cleansed, nine offer no genuine thanks at all.

Our Lord was grieved at these ungrateful lepers and said, "Were there not ten cleansed? but where are the nine? There are not found that returned to give glory to God, save this stranger'' (Luke 17:17-18). Will He have to ask the same question regarding any of us? We may have often wondered at the ingratitude of those nine cleansed lepers. But what about our own ingratitude? Do we not continually pass by innumerable blessings without notice? Instead, we fix our eyes on what we feel to be our trials and our losses. We think and talk about these until our whole horizon is filled with them, and we almost begin to think we have no blessings at all.

Imagine how this must grieve the Lord. A child who complains about the provision his parent has made wounds that parent's heart beyond words. Some people are always complaining, nothing ever pleases them, and no kindness ever seems to be appreciated. We know how uncomfortable the company of such people makes us feel. We also know how life is brightened by the presence of one who never complains, but who finds something to be pleased with in every situation.

Far more misery than we imagine is caused in human hearts by the grumblings of those they love. God's children never dream how severely they wound His heart by their continual murmuring.

It is often despairingly said of fretful, complaining individuals upon whom every care and attention has been lavished, "Will nothing ever satisfy them?" How often must God turn away, grieved by our complaints, when His love has been lavished upon us. We should try, for His sake, to be cheerful and content despite the circumstances.

A girl had to undergo very painful treatment for a serious disease. The doctors dreaded hearing her cries of pain during the procedure. But to their amazement, not even a moan escaped her lips. Instead, she smiled at her father who was with her and uttered only words of love and tenderness to him. The doctors could not understand it.

When the worst was over, one of them asked how she did it. She replied softly, "I knew how much my father loved me, and I knew how he would suffer if he saw that I suffered, so I tried to hide my suffering; and I smiled to make him think I did not mind." Can any of us do this for our heavenly Father?

Complaining During Circumstances

Job was a great complainer. We may think that if ever anyone had good reasons for complaining, Job did. His circumstances seemed to be full of hopeless misery. "My soul is weary of my life; I will leave my complaint upon myself; I will speak in the bitterness of my soul. I will say unto God, Do not condemn me; shew me wherefore thou contendest with me. Is it good unto thee that thou shouldest oppress, that thou shouldest despise the work of thine hands" (Job 10:1-3).

We can hardly be surprised at Job's complaint. And yet, if he could have seen the divine side of all his troubles, he would have known that they were permitted in the tenderest love. His trials were to bring him a revelation of God that he could not experience by other means.

If Job could have seen this outcome, he would not have uttered a single complaint. Rather, he would have given triumphant thanks for the trials which were to bring him such glorious results. If we could see in our heaviest trials the end from the beginning, we would give thanks instead of complaining.

The children of Israel were always complaining about something. They complained because they had no water. When water was supplied, they complained that it was bitter to their taste. We likewise complain because the spiritual water we have to drink seems bitter to our taste. Our souls are thirsty, and we do not like the supply that is provided. Our experiences do not quench our thirst, and our religious exercises seem dull and unsatisfying. We feel like we are in a dry and thirsty land where there is no water. We have turned from the fountain of living waters, and then we complain because the cisterns we have dug out for ourselves hold no water. (See Jeremiah 2:13.)

The Israelites complained about their food. They had so little confidence in God that they were afraid they would die of starvation. Then when the heavenly manna was provided, they complained again because they hated the taste of such light food.

We also complain about our spiritual food. Like the Israelites, we have so little confidence in God that we are afraid we will die of spiritual starvation. We complain because our preacher does not feed us or because our religious privileges are very scanty. Or we complain because we are not supplied with the same spiritual meat as others who seem to be more highly favored. We covet their circumstances or their experiences. We have asked God to feed us, and then our souls dislike the food He gives. We think it is too light to sustain or strengthen us. We have asked for bread, and we complain that He has given a stone.

The provision our divine Master has made of spiritual drink and spiritual food is always the best for us. We would be thankful for it if we realized this. The difficult part is that we must believe now, before we see the results, that the Shepherd knows the best pasture for His sheep. Surely, if we did, our hearts would be filled with thanksgiving and our mouths with praise, even in the wilderness.

The story of Jonah gives us a wonderful illustration of this. His prayer of thanksgiving out of the belly of the fish is a tremendous lesson. "I cried by reason of mine affliction unto the Lord, and he heard me; out of the belly of hell cried I, and thou heardest my voice. For thou hadst cast me into the deep, in the midst of the seas; and the floods compassed me about: all thy billows and thy waves passed over me. . . .But I will sacrifice unto thee with a voice of thanksgiving; I will pay that that I have vowed. Salvation is of the Lord" (Jonah 2:2-3,9).

No depth of misery, not even the belly of hell, is too great for the sacrifice of thanksgiving. We cannot give thanks for the misery, but we can give thanks to the Lord in the misery, just as Jonah did. No matter what our trouble, the Lord is in it somewhere. Of course, He is there to help and bless us. Therefore, when our souls faint within us because of our troubles, we have only to remember this and to thank Him for His presence and His love.

The Benefit Box

It is not because things are good that we are to thank the Lord, but because *He* is good. We are not wise enough to understand things such as true joys or sorrows. But we always know that the Lord is good. His goodness makes it absolutely certain that everything He provides or permits must be good. Therefore, we would be heartily thankful for it if only we could see it with His eyes.

In an excellent little tract called "Mrs. Pickett's Missionary Box," the story is told of a poor woman who had never done anything but complain all her life. She thought that she had no benefits to give thanks for when she received a missionary box with the words written on it, "What shall I render unto the Lord for all His benefits toward me?" She was asked by her niece, who believed in being thankful, to put a penny into the box for every blessing she could discover in her life. Here is the aunt's response:

" 'Great benefits I have!' says I, standing with my arms akimbo, an' looking that box all over. 'Guess the heathen won't get much out of me at that rate.' An' I jest made up my mind I would keep count, jest to show myself how little I did have. 'Them few pennies won't break me,' I thought, and I really seemed to kinder enjoy thinkin' over the hard times I had.

"Well, the box sat there all that week, an' I used to say it must be kinder lonesome with nothin' in it; for not a penny went into it until next mission-ary meetin' day. I was sittin' on the back steps gettin' a breath of fresh air when Mary came home an' sat down alongside o' me an' began to tell me about the meetin', an' it was all about India an' the widders there, poor creatures, an' they bein' abused, an' starved, an' not let to think for them-selves—you know all about it better'n I do!—an' before I thought, I up an' said—

" 'Well, if I be a widder, I'm thankful I'm where I kin earn my own livin', an' no thanks to nobody an' no one to interfere!'

"Then Mary, she laughed an' said there was my first benefit. Well, that sorter tickled me, for I thought a woman must be pretty hard up for bene-fits when she had to go clear off to India to find them, an' I dropped in one penny, an' it rattled round a few days without any company. I used to shake it every time I passed the shelf, an' the

241

thought of them poor things in India kep' a-comin' up before me, an' I really was glad when I got a new boarder for me best room, an' felt as if I'd oughter put in another. An' next meetin', Mary she told me about China, an' I thought about that till I put in another because I warn't a Chinese. An' all the while I felt kinder proud of how little there was in that box. Then one day, when I got a chance to turn a little penny sellin' eggs, which I warn't in the habit of, Mary brought the box in where I was countin' of my money an' says—

" 'A penny for your benefit, Aunt Mirandy.'

"I says, 'This ain't the Lord's benefit.'

"She answered, 'If 'tain't His, whose is it?' An' she begun to hum over somethin' out of one of the poetry books that she was always a readin' of—

　　　God's grace is the only grace,
　　　And all grace is the grace of God.

"Well, I dropped in my penny, an' them words kep' ringin' in my ears, till I couldn't help puttin' more to it, on account of some other things I never thought of callin' the Lord's benefits before. An' by that time, what with Mary's tellin' me about them meetin's, an' me most always findin' somethin' to put in a penny for, to be thankful that I warn't it, an' what with gettin' interested about it all, and sorter searchin' round a little now and then to think of somethin' or other to put a penny in for, there really come to be quite a few pennies in the box, an' it didn't rattle near so much when I shook it."

There is a Psalm which I call our Benefit Psalm. It is Psalm 103, and it recounts some of the benefits the Lord has bestowed upon us. We are urged not to forget them. "Bless the Lord, O my soul, and forget not all His benefits" (Psalm 103:2). Our dear sister's Benefit Box had taught her something of the meaning of this Psalm. All her life she had been forgetting the benefits the Lord has bestowed upon her, but now she was beginning to remember them.

Have we begun to remember ours? If during the past year we had kept count of those benefits for which we had actually given thanks, how many pennies would our boxes contain?

Rejecting The Wrappings

We sometimes sing a hymn of thanksgiving with the chorus, "Count your many blessings, name them one by one, and it will surprise you what the Lord has done." I wonder whether any of us who sing it so heartily have ever kept the slightest record of our blessings or even knew that we had any.

The trouble is that God's gifts often come to us wrapped up in such rough coverings that we are tempted to reject them as worthless. Or, the messengers who bring them come in the guise of enemies, and we want to shut the door against them. But we lose far more than we know when we reject even the most unlikely blessing.

We are commanded to "enter into his gates with

thanksgiving, and into his courts with praise" (Psalm 100:4.) The giving of thanks is the key that opens these gates more quickly than anything else. The next time you feel dead, cold, and low-spirited, begin to praise and thank the Lord. List the benefits He has bestowed upon you and thank Him heartily for each one. See if your spirits do not begin to rise and your heart begin to warm.

Sometimes, you may feel too disheartened to pray. Then try giving thanks instead. Before you know it, you will find yourself rejoicing in the abundance of His lovingkindnesses and His tender mercies.

One of my friends told me that her little boy flatly refused to say his prayers one night. He said there was not a single thing in all the world he wanted, and he did not see what was the good of asking for things that he did not want. His mother said, "Well, Charlie, suppose then we give thanks for all the things you have got."

The idea pleased the child, and he willingly knelt down and began to give thanks. He thanked God for his marbles and for a new top that had just been given him and for his strong legs that could run so far. He thanked God that he was not blind like a little boy he knew and for his kind father and mother and for his nice bed and for one after another of his blessings. The list grew so long that at last he said he believed he would never get done. And when finally they rose from their knees, he said to his mother, with his face shining with happiness, "Oh, mother, I never knew before how perfectly splendid God is!" If we followed the example of this little boy, we too would discover, as never before, the goodness of our God.

The Glory Of The Lord

It is very important to notice how much thanksgiving had to do with the building of the Temple. When they collected the treasures for the Temple, David gave thanks to the Lord for enabling them to do it. When the Temple was finished, they gave thanks again. And then a wonderful thing happened as the trumpeters and singers were praising and thanking the Lord. The house of the Lord was filled with a cloud, so that the priests could not stand to minister because of it. The glory of the Lord·had filled the house of God.

When the people praised and gave thanks, the house was filled with the glory of the Lord. We may be sure that the reason our hearts are not filled with the glory of the Lord more often is because we do not usually make our voices heard in praising and thanking Him.

If the giving of thanks is the way to open the gates of the Lord, complaining closes these gates. "The Lord cometh with ten thousand of his saints. To execute judgment upon all, and to convince all that are ungodly among them. . .of all their hard speeches which ungodly sinners have spoken against him. These are murmurers, complainers, walking after their own lusts" (Jude 14-16).

People who are murmurers and complainers make more hard speeches against the Lord than they would like to admit. We should not be surprised that the judgment of God, instead of the glory of God, is their reward.

There are hundreds of Bible passages concerning praising and thanking the Lord. It is amazing how they can have been so persistently ignored. Read the last seven Psalms and form your own opinion. They are simply overflowing with a list of the things for which we are called upon to give thanks. All of them are things relating to the character and the ways of God, which we dare not dispute. They are blessings which we continually forget because we take them for granted and never give thanks for them.

Beginning Your Praise-Life

The psalmist knew how to count his many blessings and name them one by one. He would have us do likewise. Try it, and you will indeed be surprised to see what the Lord has done. Go over these Psalms verse by verse and blessing by blessing. See if, like the little boy of our story, you confess that you never knew before how splendid God is.

The last verse of the book of Psalms, taken in connection with the vision of John in Revelation, is very significant. The psalmist says, "Let everything that hath breath praise the Lord" (Psalm 150:6). In Revelation, John, who declares himself to be our brother and companion in tribulation, tells us, "And every creature which is in heaven, and on the earth, and under the earth, and such as are in the sea, and all that are in them, heard I saying, Blessing, and honour, and glory, and power, be unto him that sitteth upon the throne, and unto the Lamb forever and ever" (Revelation 5:13).

The time for universal praise is sure to come some day. Let us begin to do our part now!

Chapter 16

CONFORMED TO THE IMAGE OF CHRIST

"For whom he did foreknow, he also did pre-destinate to be conformed to the image of his son, that he might be the firstborn among many brethren"—Romans 8:29.

God's ultimate purpose in our creation is that we be conformed to the image of Christ. Christ is the firstborn among many brethren, and His brethren are to be like Him. Throughout the discipline and training period of our lives, we should keep this goal in view.

God said in the beginning, "Let us make man in our image, after our likeness" (Genesis 1:26). We cannot imagine that He meant we were to be made in the image or likeness of His body. He must have meant that man was to be made in the image or likeness of His nature and character. He could not have meant that man, when first created, was to be created completely in this image, but only that he was to begin, as all adult life is begun, in helpless, ignorant babyhood.

Just as an architect could say of a great building, when only the foundation stones were in place, "This is a cathedral," so God could say of man, "This is My image," although as yet only the foundation stones of this image were laid. We are told in 1 Corinthians 15:47 that, "the first man is of the earth earthy."

It was only the foundation stones of God's final purpose for man which were laid at man's creation. This is plain from the fact that man had no knowledge of the difference between right and wrong. He was, therefore, in a very undeveloped state. It could not possibly be said that he was in the likeness of God in this respect. But the embryo of God's image was in man, and God's purpose in regard to him began to be accomplished then. It has gone on, in a grand process of growth, ever since—both in the individual and in the race.

Our Pattern

Christ is the pattern of what each one of us is to be when finished. We are predestined to be conformed to His image, in order that He might be the firstborn among many brethren. We are to be partakers of the divine nature with Christ, filled with His Spirit, and sharing His resurrection life. We are to be one with Him, as He is one with the Father. The glory that God gave to Him, He is to give to us. When all this is brought to pass, only then will God's purpose in our creation be fully accomplished. We will stand in His image and likeness.

Our likeness to His image is an accomplished fact in the mind of God. We are, so to speak, in the factory as yet, and the great Master Workman is busy with us. "It doth not yet appear what we shall be: but we know that, when he shall appear, we shall be like him; for we shall see him as he is" (1 John 3:2).

"And so it is written, The first man Adam was made a living soul; the last Adam was made a quickening spirit. Howbeit that was not first which is spiritual, but that which is natural; and afterward that which is spiritual. The first man is of the earth, earthy: the second man is the Lord from heaven. As is the earthy, such are they also that are earthy: and as is the heavenly, such are they also that are heavenly. And as we have borne the image of the earthy, we shall also bear the image of the heavenly" (1 Corinthians 15:45-49).

The grand process of Christian development is set forth here. "The first man Adam was made a living soul." This expression *living soul* means in the Hebrew the same thing as *living creature* which was the description given of the animal kingdom. Man, therefore, when first created, was simply "of the earth earthy," since he had no conscience nor any knowledge of the difference between right and wrong.

The serpent tempted man to eat of the tree of the knowledge of good and evil, and said, "For God doth know that in the day ye eat thereof, then your eyes shall be opened, and ye shall be as gods, knowing good and evil" (Genesis 3:5). After Adam and Eve had eaten of the tree, the Lord confirmed this and said, "Behold, the man is become as one of us, to know good and evil" (Genesis 3:22). Instead of this being a fall out of a higher state into a lower, as is so often thought, it actually was a step upward out of a lower stage of development into a higher.

As one of us—this could not have been said of him before. It marked a distinct step upward in his development. The baby's innocence that knows no difference between right and wrong may be a beautiful thing in its place. But it becomes idiotic when it continues on into manhood. Man, who was destined to grow up into Christ in all things, needed first of all to become acquainted with the difference between right and wrong. No progress was possible until this took place.

The first step in man's spiritual development had now been taken. Man discovered the difference between right and wrong and began to develop a spiritual nature, a nature which God Himself declared was like His own. From that moment on, the conflict between the spiritual man and the natural man has never ceased.

"For the flesh lusteth against the Spirit, and the Spirit against the flesh: and these are contrary the one to the other: so that ye cannot do the things that ye would" (Galatians 5:17).

"For they that are after the flesh do mind the things of the flesh; but they that are after the Spirit the things of the Spirit. For to be carnally minded is death; but to be spiritually minded is life and peace. Because the carnal mind is enmity against God: for it is not subject to the law of God, neither indeed can be" (Romans 8:5-7).

It is interesting to see that spiritual growth, which was begun in Genesis, is declared to be completed in Revelation. The "one like unto the Son of Man" gave John this significant message to the overcomers. "Him that overcometh will I make a pillar in the temple of my God, and he shall go no more out: and I will write upon him the name of my God, and the name of the city of my God, which is the new Jerusalem, which cometh down out of heaven from my God: and I will write upon him my new name" (Revelation 3:12).

Since name always means character in the Bible, this message can only mean that at last God's purpose is accomplished, and the spiritual development of man is completed. He has been made into what God intended from the first, so truly into His likeness and image that he will have the name of God written upon him!

Complete Oneness With God

Words fail in the face of such a glorious destiny as this! But our Lord foreshadowed it when He prayed for His brethren, "That they all may be one; as thou, Father, art in me, and I in thee, that they also may be one in us: that the world may believe that thou hast sent me. And the glory which thou gavest me I have given them; that they may be one, even as we are one: I in them, and thou in me, that they may be made perfect in one" (John 17:21-23). Could oneness be closer or more complete?

Paul also foreshadows this glorious communion when he declares, "If so be that we suffer with him, we may also be glorified together. For I reckon that the sufferings of this present time are not worthy to be compared with the glory which shall be revealed in us" (Romans 8:17-18).

The whole creation waits for the revealing of this glory. Paul goes on to say that the "earnest expectation of the creature waiteth for the manifestation of the sons of God." And he adds, "And not only they, but ourselves also, which have the first fruits of the Spirit, even we ourselves groan within ourselves, waiting for the adoption, to wit, the redemption of our body" (Romans 8:19-23).

In view of such a glorious destiny, will we not cheerfully welcome the processes, however painful they may be, by which we are to reach it? And should we not strive eagerly and earnestly to work with God in helping to bring it about?

He is the great Master Builder, but He wants our cooperation in building up the fabric of our characters. He exhorts us to be prudent in how we build. At every moment of our lives, we are engaged in this building. Sometimes we build with gold and silver and precious stones, and sometimes we build with wood and hay and stubble. We are solemnly warned that every man's work is to be made manifest, "for the day shall declare it, because it shall be revealed by fire" (1 Corinthians 3:13). There is no escaping this. We cannot hope when that day comes to conceal our wood and hay and stubble, no matter how successfully we may have managed to do so previously.

There is no more solemn passage in the whole Bible than Galatians 6:7 which says, "Be not deceived; God is not mocked: for whatsoever a man soweth, that shall he also reap. For he that soweth to the flesh shall of the flesh reap corruption; but he that soweth to the Spirit shall of the Spirit reap life everlasting."

It is the certainty of this that is so awe inspiring. It is far worse than any arbitrary punishment, for punishment can sometimes be averted. But there is no possibility of altering the work of a natural law such as this.

In a Catechism, I saw the following questions and answers—

Q. What is the reward for generosity?

A. More generosity.

Q. What is the punishment for meanness?

A. More meanness.

No Catechism ever spoke more truly. All of us know it for ourselves.

In the parable of the talents, our Lord illustrates this law. The condemnation on the unfaithful servant may have sometimes seemed to us unfair, but the servant was only reaping what he had sowed. "Take therefore the talent from him, and give it unto him which hath ten talents. For unto every one that hath shall be given, and he shall have abundance: but from him that hath not, shall be taken away even that which he hath" (Matthew 25:28-29). This is no arbitrary pronouncement, but it is simply a revelation of the nature of things, from which none of us can escape.

Beholding His Glory

In order to be laborers together with God, we must not only build with His materials, but also by His processes. Of these we are often very ignorant. Our idea of building is of hard laborious work. God's idea is far different. Paul tells us what it is. "But we all, with open face beholding as in a glass the glory of the Lord, are changed into the same image from glory to glory, even as by the Spirit of the Lord" (2 Corinthians 3:18).

Our work is to "behold," and, as we behold, the Lord brings about the marvelous transformation. We are "changed into the same image by the Spirit of the Lord." This means to behold, not in our earthly sense of merely looking at a thing, but in the divine sense of seeing the thing. We are to behold with our spiritual eyes the glory of the Lord, and we are to continue beholding it. The glory of the Lord does not mean, however, a great heavenly halo. The real glory of the Lord is the glory of what He is and of what He does, the glory of His character. This is what we are to behold.

Let me give an illustration. If someone offends me, I am tempted to get angry and retaliate. But instead, I look at Christ and think of what He would have done. I meditate upon His gentleness and meekness and His love for the offending one. As I look, I begin to want to be like Him, and I ask in faith that I may be made a "partaker of His nature." Anger and revenge die out of my heart, and I love my enemy and long to serve him.

It is by this sort of beholding Christ that we are to be changed into His image. The nearer we stay to Him, the more rapid the change will be.

There is a wonderful mirror which is called the parabolic mirror. It consists of a hollow cone lined with a mirror all over its inside surface. It has the power to focus rays of light in different degrees of intensity, in proportion to the increasing nearness to its meeting-point at the top of the cone. The power intensifies as the terminal point is approached. It has been discovered by science that at a certain stage in this advance toward the interior point all the sides of the mirror meet in absolute oneness. The power of the focus concentrates all the light-giving properties of the sun's rays into such an intense brilliancy and makes visible things never before discerned by the human eye. It renders even flesh transparent and enables us to see through the outer covering of our bodies to the inner operations beneath.

Advancing a little further into the interior of our mirror, the heat properties of the sun's rays are so concentrated that enough heat is generated to melt iron in sixteen seconds. It can also separate the alloys of gold, leaving only the solid globule of the pure metal, in fourteen seconds.

Advancing further still, the photographing properties of the sunlight are so concentrated that they stamp a permanent image of the mirror upon anything that is passed through the focus.

Advancing still further, nearly to the point of oneness, the magnetizing powers of light are so concentrated that anything exposed to it for a single instant becomes a powerful magnet, drawing all things to itself.

I am not a scientist, but this illustration will serve as an allegory to show the progress of the soul, as it is changed from glory to glory into His image.

Our Process Of Change

First, as we behold as in a mirror the glory of the Lord, we come to the light focus which reveals our sinfulness and our need. "Then spake Jesus again unto them, saying, I am the light of the world: he that followeth me shall not walk in darkness, but shall have the light of life" (John 8:12).

Second, as we draw closer, we reach the heat focus, where all our dross is burned up. "For he is like a refiner's fire, and like fullers' soap: And shall sit as a refiner and purifier of silver: and he shall purify the sons of Levi, and purge them as gold and silver, that they may offer unto the Lord an offering in righteousness" (Malachi 3:2-3).

Third, as we draw closer still, we come to the photographing focus, where the image of Christ is impressed upon our souls, and we are made like Him because we see Him as He is. "We know that, when he shall appear, we shall be like him; for we shall see him as he is" (1 John 3:2).

Fourth and finally, as we come to the point of oneness, we reach the magnetic focus. Our character is so conformed to Christ that men, seeing it, will be drawn to glorify our Father which is in heaven.

If we want to be conformed to the image of Christ, we must grow ever closer to Him. We must become better acquainted with His character and His ways. We must look at things through His eyes and judge all things by His standards.

It is not by effort or by wrestling that this conformity is to be accomplished. Rather, it is by assimilation. According to a natural law, we grow like those with whom we associate. The stronger character always exercises the controlling influence. Divine law is all one with natural law, only working in a higher sphere and with more unhindered power. It should not seem mysterious to us that we become like Christ by a spiritual union with Him.

The Indwelling Christ

This union with Christ cannot come by our own efforts, no matter how strenuous they may be. Christ is to "dwell in your hearts by faith" (Ephesians 3:17), and He can dwell there in no other way. Paul, when he tells us that he was crucified with Christ, says, "nevertheless I live; yet not I, but Christ liveth in me: and the life which I now live in the flesh I live by the faith of the Son of God, who loved me, and gave himself for me" (Galatians 2:20).

"Christ liveth in me"—this is the transforming secret. If Christ lives in me, His life must be manifested in my mortal flesh. Therefore, I cannot fail to be changed from glory to glory into His image.

Our Lord's teaching about this is very clear. "Abide in me, and I in you. As the branch cannot bear fruit of itself, except it abide in the vine; no more can ye, except ye abide in me. I am the vine, ye are the branches: He that abideth in me, and I in him, the same bringeth forth much fruit: for without me ye can do nothing" (John 15:4-5).

If we abide in Him, and He in us, we can no more help bringing forth much fruit than can the branches of a flourishing vine. In the very nature of things the fruit must come.

But we cannot take the old man into Christ. We must put off the old man with his deeds before we can put on the Lord Jesus Christ. In writing to the Colossians, Paul bases his exhortations to a life of holiness on the fact that they had done this. "Lie not one to another, seeing that ye have put off the old man with his deeds; And have put on the new man, which is renewed in knowledge after the image of him that created him" (Colossians 3:9-10).

Sin must disappear at the incoming of Christ. A soul that is not prepared to surrender all that is contrary to His will cannot hope to welcome Him. The old man must be put off if the new man is to reign. But both the putting off and the putting on must be done by faith. There is no other way.

We must move our personality, our ego, and our will out of self and into Christ. We must consider ourselves to be dead to self and alive only to God. "Likewise reckon ye also yourselves to be dead indeed unto sin, but alive unto God through Jesus Christ our Lord. Neither yield ye your members as instruments of unrighteousness unto sin; but yield yourselves unto God, as those that are alive from the dead, and your members as instruments of righteousness unto God" (Romans 6:11-13).

The same kind of faith which brings the forgiveness of sins within our grasp also brings this union with Christ. To those who do not understand the law of faith, this will no doubt be as great a mystery as the secrets of gravity were before the law of gravity was discovered. But to those who understand it, the law of faith works as unerringly and as definitely as the law of gravity.

No one can read the seventh chapter of Hebrews

and fail to see that faith is an all-conquering force. I believe it is the creative force of the universe. It is the higher law that controls all the lower laws beneath it. What looks like a miracle is simply the working of the higher controlling law of faith.

The Law Of Creation

Faith is the law of creation—"Through faith we understand that the worlds were framed by the word of God, so that things which are seen were not made of things which do appear" (Hebrews 11:3). We are told in Psalm 33:9, "For he spake and it was done, he commanded and it stood fast."

Our Lord tells us that if we have faith, we can do the same. "And Jesus answering saith unto them, Have faith in God. For verily I say unto you, That whosoever shall say unto this mountain, Be thou removed, and be thou cast into the sea; and shall not doubt in his heart, but shall believe that those things which he saith shall come to pass; he shall have whatsoever he saith. Therefore I say unto you, what things soever ye desire, when ye pray, believe that ye receive them, and ye shall have them" (Mark 11:22-24).

Faith, we are told, "calleth those things which be not as though they were." Calling them brings them into being. Therefore, we may not see any tangible sign of change when by faith we put off the old man, which is corrupt according to the deceitful lusts, and by faith put on the new man which God created in righteousness and true holiness. Yet, it has been done, and faith has accomplished it. Those souls who abandon the self life and give themselves up to the Lord to be fully possessed by Him find that He takes possession of the inner springs of their being. He works there to will and to do great things in their lives.

Paul prayed for the Ephesians that "Christ might dwell in your hearts by faith" (Ephesians 3:17). This is the whole secret of being conformed to His image. If Christ lives in my heart, I must necessarily be Christlike. I cannot be unkind or irritable or self-seeking or dishonest. Rather, His gentleness and sweetness and tender compassion and loving submission to the will of His Father must be manifested in my daily walk and conversation.

We will not be fully changed into the image of Christ until He appears and we see Him face to face. But meanwhile, the life of Jesus is to be "made manifest in our mortal flesh" (2 Corinthians 4:11). Is it made manifest in ours? Are we so conformed to the image of Christ that men, in seeing us, see a glimpse of Him also?

A minister's wife told me that when they had moved to a new place, her little boy came in after the first afternoon of play and exclaimed joyfully, "Oh, Mother, I have found such a lovely, good little girl to play with here that I never want to go away again."

"I am very glad, darling," said the loving mother, happy because of her child's happiness, "what is the little girl's name?"

"Oh," replied the child with a sudden solemnity, "I think her name is Jesus."

"Why, Frank!" exclaimed the horrified mother, "what do you mean?"

"Well, Mother," he said apologetically, "she was so lovely that I did not know what else she could be called but Jesus."

Are our lives so Christlike that anyone could think this way about us? Is it apparent to all around us that we have been with Jesus? Is it not, sadly, often just the contrary? Are some of us so irritable and uncomfortable in our daily lives that exactly the opposite thing would have to be said about us?

Paul says we are to be "the epistle of Christ ministered by us, written not with ink, but with the Spirit of the living God; not in tables of stone, but in fleshy tables of the heart" (2 Corinthians 3:3). If every child of God would begin today to be an epistle of Christ, living a truly Christlike life, in less than a month, the churches would be crowded by inquirers. People would come in to see what was the religion that could transform human nature into something divine.

The world is full of unbelievers, and nothing will convince them but the facts of Christianity which they cannot disprove. We must meet them with transformed lives. If they see that once we were resentful, but now we are sweet; once we were proud, but now we are humble; once we were fretful, but now we are patient and calm; if we are able to testify that it is Christ who has brought about this change, they cannot help but be impressed.

Convincing Transformations

A Christian man who, on account of his earnest work, had gained a great reputation for his devotion, had unfortunately gained an equally great reputation for a bad temper and a sharp tongue. But at last, for some reason which no one could understand, a change seemed to come over him. His temper and his tongue became as sweet and as gentle as they had before been violent and sharp. His friends watched and wondered. Before long one of them approached him on the subject and asked him if he had changed his faith. "No," replied the man, "I have not changed my faith, but I have at last let my faith change me."

How much has our faith changed us? It is very easy to have a church religion or a prayer-meeting religion or a Christian-work religion. But it is a different thing to have an everyday faith. To show love at home is one of the most vital parts of Christianity, but it is also one far too rare. It is not at all uncommon to find Christians who do their righteousness before outsiders to be seen by men. But they fail to show love or joy at home.

I knew a father who was powerful in prayer at the weekly prayer meeting and impressive in exhortation. The whole church was much edified by his example. But when he went home after the meetings, he was so cross and ugly that his wife and family were afraid to say a word in his presence.

"And when thou prayest, thou shalt not be as the hypocrites are: for they love to pray standing in the synagogues and in the corners of the streets, that they may be seen of men. Verily I say unto you, They have their reward" (Matthew 6:5). What we do to be seen of men, is seen of men, and that is all there is to it. There is no conformity to the image of Christ in this sort of righteousness.

The righteousness that is Christlike is the righteousness that bears everyday trials cheerfully and is patient under home irritations. It returns good for evil and meets all the friction of daily life with sweetness and gentleness. It suffers long and is kind; it does not envy others or boast about itself. It does not seek its own, is not easily provoked, and thinks no evil. It bears all things, believes all things, hopes all things, endures all things. This is what it means to be conformed to the image of Christ! Do we know anything of such righteousness as this?

True Christian Living

We sometimes talk about performing what we call our "religious duties," meaning by this expression our church services or devotions or our Christian work of one sort or another. We never dream that it is far more our "religious duty" to be Christlike in our daily walk and conversation than even to be faithful in these other things, desirable as they may be in themselves.

The righteousness of the Scribes and Pharisees was a righteousness of words and phrases and of ceremonial observances. This is often very impressive to outsiders. But because it was nothing more, our Lord condemns it saying, "Woe unto you, scribes and Pharisees, hypocrites! for ye pay tithe of mint and anise and cummin, and have omitted the weightier matters of the law, judgment, mercy, and faith: these ought ye to have done, and not to leave the other undone. Woe unto you, scribes and Pharisees, hypocrites! for ye are like unto whited sepulchres, which indeed appear beautiful outward, but are within full of dead men's bones, and all of uncleanness. . . .Even so ye also outwardly appear righteous unto men, but within ye are full of hypocrisy and iniquity" (Matthew 23:23, 27-28).

It is very easy to say beautiful things about the Christian life, but to live what we say is a different matter. I know a Sunday school teacher who had been teaching her students a great deal about casting all their cares on the Lord and trusting Him in times of trial. The students had been very much impressed. But when trouble came into the life of this teacher, her students watched while it lasted. To their amazement and distress, they saw her fretting and worrying and complaining. She was acting just as if there was no God to trust or as if His ways were not ways of love and goodness.

It was an object lesson to those children that undid all the good which that teacher's previous teaching had seemed likely to accomplish. One of them, who was very observant, said to me triumphantly, "I wondered if it could be true what she was telling us about how we might trust the Lord for everything; now I see it was only talk, for she doesn't do it herself."

An ill-tempered, discouraged, gloomy, doubting, complaining, demanding Christian, or one with a sharp tongue or a bitter spirit, a Christian, in short, who is not Christlike, may preach to the winds with as much hope of success as to preach to his own family or friends who see him as he is.

There is no escape from this inevitable law. If we want our loved ones to trust the Lord, volumes of talk about it will not be nearly as convincing to them as the sight of a little sincere trust on our own part in the time of need. The longest prayer and the loudest preaching are of no use in any family circle, however well they may do in the pulpit, unless the preacher lives the things he preaches.

Being Made Perfect

Some Christians seem to think that the fruits which the Bible calls for are some form of outward religious work, such as holding meetings, visiting the poor, or supporting charitable institutions. The fact is that the Bible scarcely mentions these at all as fruits of the Spirit. "But the fruit of the

Spirit is love, joy, peace, longsuffering, gentleness, goodness, faith, meekness, temperance'' (Galatians 5:22-23).

A Christlike character must be the fruit of Christ's indwelling. Other things will no doubt be the outcome of this character. But first comes the character or all the rest is a hollow sham. A writer once said: "A man can never be more than his character makes him. A man can never do more nor better than deliver or embody that which is his character. Nothing valuable can come out of a man that is not first in the man. Character must stand behind and back up everything—the sermon, the poem, the picture, the book. None of them is worth a straw without it."

In order to become conformed to the image of Christ, we must be made partakers of the divine nature. Our tastes, our wishes, and our purposes will then become like Christ's tastes, wishes, and purposes. We will exchange eyes with Him and see things as He sees them. This is inevitable; for where the divine nature is, its fruits cannot fail to be manifest.

"But," you may ask, "do you really mean to say that, in order to be made partakers of the divine nature, we must cease from our own efforts entirely, and by faith put on Christ? Must we simply let Him live in us and work in us to will and to do of His good pleasure? And do you believe He will then actually do it?"

To this I answer most emphatically, "Yes, I

mean just that!" If we abandon ourselves entirely to Him, He comes to abide in us and is Himself our life. We must commit our whole lives to Him, our thoughts, our words, our daily work, our sitting down, and our rising up.

By faith we must abandon ourselves and move over into Christ and abide in Him. By faith we must put off the old man, and by faith we must put on the new man. By faith we must consider ourselves as dead to sin and alive to God. By faith we must realize that our daily life is Christ living in us. Ceasing from our own works, we must allow Him to work in us to will and to do His good pleasure.

It is no longer truth about Him that will fill our hearts, but it is the living, loving, glorious Christ Himself. He will, if we let Him, make us His dwelling place. He will reign and rule within us. "Therefore if any man be in Christ, he is a new creature: old things are passed away; behold, all things are become new" (2 Corinthians 5:17).

It was no mere figure of speech when our Lord said to His disciples, "Be ye therefore perfect, even as your Father which is in heaven is perfect" (Matthew 5:48). In the letter to the Hebrews, we are shown how it is to be brought about. "Now the God of peace, that brought again from the dead our Lord Jesus, that great shepherd of the sheep, through the blood of the everlasting covenant, Make you perfect in every good work to do his will, working in you that which is wellpleasing in his sight, through Jesus Christ; to whom be glory forever and ever. Amen" (Hebrews 13:20-21).

By His working in us, and not by our working in ourselves, this purpose of God in our creation will be accomplished. It may look to some of us as though we are too far removed from any conformity to the image of Christ for such a transformation ever to take place. But we must remember that our Maker is not finished with us yet. The day will come when the work begun in Genesis will be finished in Revelation. All of creation will be delivered from the bondage of corruption into the glorious liberty of the children of God.

"For we know that the whole creation groaneth and travaileth in pain together until now. And not only they, but ourselves also, which have the firstfruits of the Spirit, even we ourselves groan within ourselves, waiting for the adoption, to wit, the redemption of our body" (Romans 8:22-23).

Chapter 17

GOD IS ENOUGH

"My soul, wait thou only upon God; for my expectation is from him. He only is my rock and my salvation: He is my defence; I shall not be moved. In God is my salvation and my glory: the rock of my strength, and my refuge is in God"— Psalm 62:5-7.

The last and greatest lesson that the soul has to learn is the fact that God, and God alone, is enough for all its needs. This is the lesson that all His dealings with us are meant to teach. This is the crowning discovery of our whole Christian life. *God is enough!*

We have been considering some aspects of the character and the ways of God, as revealed to us in the Lord Jesus Christ. We have also looked at some of the mistakes which prevent us from appropriating the fullness that is ours in Him.

If God is indeed the God of all comfort; if He is our Shepherd; if He is truly our Father; if all the many aspects we have been studying of His character and His ways are true, then we must conclude that He is, in Himself alone, enough for all our possible needs. Therefore, we may safely rest in Him, absolutely and forever.

Most Christians have sung these words in one of our most familiar hymns—

> "Thou, O Christ, art all I want,
> More than all in Thee I find."

But, I doubt whether all of us could honestly say that the words have expressed our true experience. Christ has not been all we want. We have wanted a great many things in addition to Him. We have wanted fervent feelings about Him or realizations of His presence with us or an interior revelation of His love. Or else we have demanded satisfactory doctrine or successful Christian work rather than Him alone. These things, we think, will give us a personal claim upon Him.

In reality, Christ Himself, Christ alone, without the addition of any of our experiences concerning Him, has not been enough for us, in spite of all our singing. We do not even see how it is possible that He could be enough.

The psalmist said in those old days, "My soul, wait thou only upon God; for my expectation is from him" (Psalm 62:5). But now the Christian says, "My soul, wait thou upon my sound doctrines, for my expectation is from them;" or "My soul, wait thou on my good feelings, upon my righteous works, upon my fervent prayers, or upon my earnest striving, for my expectation is from these."

Waiting On God

To wait upon God seems for some to be one of the most unsafe things they can do. To have their expectation from Him alone seems like building on the sand. They reach out on every side for something to depend on. Not until everything else fails will they put their trust in God alone.

George MacDonald says, "We look upon God as our last and feeblest resource. We only go to Him when we have nowhere else to go. And then we learn that the storms of life have driven us, not upon the rocks, but into the desired haven."

No soul can be at rest until it has been forced to depend on the Lord alone. As long as our expectation is from other things, nothing but disappointment awaits us. Feelings change with our changing circumstances, and doctrines and dogmas may be upset. Christian work may come to nothing. Prayers may seem to lose their fervency. Promises may seem to fail. Everything that we have believed in or depended upon may seem to be swept away, and only God is left.

We say sometimes, "If I could only find a promise to fit my case, I could then be at rest." But promises may be misunderstood or misapplied. At the moment we are leaning upon them, they may seem to fail us. But the Promiser, who is behind His promises and is infinitely more than His promises, can never fail or change. The little child does not need to have any promises from his mother to make him content; he has his mother, and she is enough. His mother is better than a thousand promises.

In our highest ideal of love or friendship, promises do not enter the picture. One person may love to make promises, just as our Lord does, but the other does not need them. The personality of the friend is better than all their promises. And if every promise was wiped out of the Bible, we would still have God left, and God would be enough. Only God Himself, just as He is, without the addition of anything on our part, whether it be feelings, experiences, good works, sound doctrines, or any other thing either outward or inward; "He only is my rock and my salvation: He is my defence; I shall not be moved" (Psalm 62:6).

I do not mean by this that we are not to have feelings, experiences, revelations, good works, or sound doctrines. We may have all of these, but they must be the result of our faith and never the cause. They can never be depended upon as being any indication of our spiritual condition. They are all things that change and are dependent upon the state of our health or the condition of our surroundings.

If we rely upon any of these things in the slightest degree, as the foundation of our confidence or our joy, we are sure to be defeated. We are to hold ourselves absolutely independent of them all, resting only in the grand, magnificent fact that God is alive and that He is our Savior. Our spiritual life will prosper just as well and be just as triumphant without these personal experiences or personal doings as with them.

We will find God to be sufficient for all our needs, whether we are in a desert or in a fertile valley. We will say with the prophet, "Although the fig tree shall not blossom, neither shall fruit be in the vines; the labour of the olive shall fail, and the field shall yield no meat; the flock shall be cut off from the fold, and there shall be no herd in the stall; Yet I will rejoice in the Lord, I will joy in the God of my salvation" (Habakkuk 3:17-18).

The soul is made for this and can never find rest with anything less. God is often obliged to deprive us of all joy in something else in order that He may force us to find our joy only in Him. It is good to rejoice in His promises or to rejoice in the revelations He may have granted us or in the experiences we may have realized. But rejoicing in the Promiser alone, even without promises or experiences or revelations, is the crowning point of the Christian life. This is the only place where we can know the peace which passes all understanding.

God's Feeling For Us

We often consider all of our own additions to the spiritual life as being the spiritual life itself. It is hard to detach ourselves from them. We think that the Lord cannot mean anything to us unless we find in ourselves something to assure us of His love and His care. When we talk about finding our all in Him, we generally mean that we find it in our feelings or our views about Him. If we feel a glow of love toward Him, then we say heartily that He is enough; but when this glow fades, as sooner or later it is almost sure to do, then we no longer feel that we have found our all in Him. This shows that it is not the Lord who satisfies us, but our own feelings about the Lord. We are not conscious of this, however. When our feelings fail, we think it is the Lord who has failed, and we are plunged into darkness.

Perhaps an illustration may help us to see it more clearly. Let us think of a man accused of a crime, standing before a judge. Which would be the concern of the moment for that man: his own feelings toward the judge or the judge's feelings toward him? Would he spend his time watching his own emotions? Or would he watch the judge and try to discover from his looks or his words whether or not to expect a favorable decision?

Of course, the man's own feelings are not of the slightest account in the matter. Only the opinions and feelings of the judge are worth a moment's thought. The man might have all the "glows" and all the "experiences" conceivable, but these would mean absolutely nothing. Everything depends upon the judge only. This is what we call a self-evident fact.

In the same way, we cannot help seeing that the only important thing in our relationship with the Lord is not our feelings toward Him, but His feelings toward us. Our sufficiency cannot possibly be of ourselves, but it must be of the one upon whom our fate depends. "Not that we are sufficient of ourselves to think any thing as of ourselves; but our sufficiency is of God" (2 Corinthians 3:5).

This is what I mean by God being enough. We find in Him, His existence and His character, all that we can possibly want for everything. *God is.* This must be our answer to every question and every cry of need. If there is any lack in the One who has saved us, nothing that we can do will begin to make up for it. If there is no lack in Him, then He, of Himself, and in Himself, is enough.

I believe that this is the secret of permanent deliverance from all the discomfort and unrest of every Christian life. Discomfort and unrest arise from strenuous but useless efforts to get up some satisfactory confidence within. For instance, you try to feel what you consider to be the proper emotions or the right amount of fervor or earnestness or at least a sufficient degree of interest in spiritual matters. Because none of these things are ever satisfactory (and never will be), it is impossible for your Christian life to be anything but uncomfortable.

But if we see that all salvation depends on the Lord alone, and if we learn that He is able and willing to do for us "exceeding abundantly above all we can ask or think" (Ephesians 3:20), then peace and comfort cannot fail to reign supreme. Everything depends upon whether the Lord, in and of Himself, is enough for our salvation, or whether other things must be added on our part to make Him sufficient.

But There Is God

There was a time in my Christian life when I was passing through a great deal of questioning and perplexity. I felt that no Christian had ever had such peculiar difficulties as mine. There happened to be staying near me for a few weeks, a lady who was considered to be a deeply spiritual Christian. I summoned up my courage one afternoon and went to see her. I poured out my troubles to her, expecting that she would take a deep interest in me and would do all she could to help me.

She listened patiently enough and did not interrupt me. But when I had finished my story and paused, expecting sympathy, she simply said, "Yes, all you say may be very true, but then, in spite of it all, there is God."

I waited a few minutes for something more, but nothing came. My friend and teacher had the attitude of having said all that was necessary.

"But," I continued, "surely you did not understand how very serious and perplexing my difficulties are."

"Oh yes, I did," replied my friend, "but then, as I tell you, there is God."

I could not induce her to make any other answer. It seemed to me most disappointing and unsatisfactory. I felt that my peculiar and difficult experiences could not be met by anything so simple as the statement, "Yes, but there is God." I knew God was there, of course, but I felt I needed something more than just God. I came to the conclusion that my friend, for all her great reputation as a spiritual teacher, was at any rate not able to handle my problems.

My need was so great, however, that I did not give up with my first attempt. I went to her again and again, always with the hope that she would sometime begin to understand the importance of my difficulties and would give me adequate help. It was of no use. I was never able to draw forth any other answer. Always to everything would come the simple reply, with an air of entirely dismissing the subject, "Yes, I know; but there is God."

At last, by power of her continual repetition, I became convinced that my friend truly believed that the mere fact of the existence of God, as the Creator and Redeemer of mankind, and of me as a member of the race, was an all-sufficient answer to every possible need. She said it so often and seemed so sure that I began to wonder whether God might be enough, even for my overwhelming and peculiar need. From wondering I came gradually to believing that, since He is my Creator and Redeemer, He must be enough. A conviction burst upon me that He truly was enough. My eyes were opened to the absolute and utter all-sufficiency of God.

My troubles disappeared, and I wondered how I could ever have been such an idiot as to be troubled by them, when all the while there was God. The Almighty and All-seeing God, the God who had created me, was on my side and eager to care for me and help me. I had found out that God was enough, and my soul was at rest.

Your Right To His Grace

But someone may say, "All this is no doubt true, and I could easily believe it, if I could only be sure it applied to me. But I am so good for nothing and so full of sin, that I do not feel as if I had any claim to such riches of grace."

If you are good-for-nothing and full of sin, you have all the more claim on the all-sufficiency of God. It is only the sinner who wants salvation that stands in the Savior's path. Jesus did not come to save the righteous, the fervent, the earnest workers, but simply and only to save sinners. Why then should we spend our time and energy in trying to create a claim to His grace which after all is no claim, but only a hindrance.

Perhaps until now, our eyes have been so exclusively fixed upon ourselves that all our interior questioning has been only regarding our own condition—Is my love for God warm enough? Am I enough in earnest? Are my feelings toward Him what they should be? Do I have enough zeal? Do I feel my need as I should? And we have been miserable because we have never been able to answer these questions to our satisfaction.

Although we do not realize it, it has been a blessing that we never could answer them satisfactorily. If we had, the self in us would have been exalted, and we would have been filled with pride.

If we want to see God, our questioning must not be about ourselves, but about Him. How does God feel toward me? Is His love for me warm enough? Has He enough zeal? Does He feel my need deeply enough? Is He sufficiently in earnest? Although these questions may seem irreverent to some, they express the doubts and fears of a great many hearts. We all know what would be the triumphant answers to such questions. No doubts could withstand their testimony. The soul that asks and answers them honestly will have the profound and absolute conviction that God is and must be enough.

Belonging To Christ

"All things are yours; Whether Paul, or Apollos, or Cephas, or the world, or life, or death, or things present, or things to come; all are yours; And ye are Christ's; and Christ is God's" (1 Corinthians 3:21-22). It would be impossible for any statement to be more all-embracing. All things are yours because you belong to Christ. It is not because you are so good and so worthy, but simply because you belong to Christ. All the things we need are part of our inheritance in Him, and they only await our claiming. Despite our needs and difficulties, there is in these "all things" a supply exceeding abundantly above all we can ask or think.

Because He is, all must go right for us. Because the mother is, all must go right, up to her ability, for her children. To the child there is, despite all that changes, the one unchangeable fact of the mother's existence. While the mother lives, the child must be cared for. While God lives, His children must be cared for as well. What else could He do, being what He is? Neglect, indifference, forgetfulness, and ignorance are all impossible to Him. He knows everything; He cares about everything; He can manage everything; and He loves us. What more could we ask?

God's saints in all ages realized that God was enough for them. Job said, out of the depths of sorrows and trials, "Though he slay me, yet will I trust in him" (Job 13:15).

David could say in the moment of his greatest anguish, "Yea, though I walk through the valley of the shadow of death, I will fear no evil: for thou art with me" (Psalm 23:4). He could say, "God is our refuge and strength, a very present help in trouble. Therefore will not we fear, though the earth be removed, and though the mountains be carried into the midst of the sea; Though the waters thereof roar and be troubled, though the mountains shake with the swelling thereof. . . .God is in the midst of her; she shall not be moved: God shall help her, and that right early'' (Psalm 46:1-3,5).

Paul could say triumphantly, in the midst of many grievous trials, "For I am persuaded, that neither death, nor life, nor angels, nor principalities, nor powers, nor things present, nor things to come, Nor height, nor depth, nor any other creature, shall be able to separate us from the love of God, which is in Christ Jesus our Lord'' (Romans 8:38-39).

Therefore, O doubting and sorrowful Christian, consider all that we have learned concerning the God of all comfort. Can you understand with Job and David and Paul and the saints of all ages, that nothing else is needed to quiet all your fears, but just this: *God is.*

After such a declaration as this, how can any of us dare to question or doubt God's love? Since He loves us, He cannot fail to help us. Do we not know by our own experience that love must pour itself out in blessing on the ones it loves? Can we not understand that God, who is love, who is even made out of love, simply cannot help blessing us. We do not need to beg Him to bless us; He simply cannot help it.

Therefore God is enough! God is enough for time. God is enough for eternity. *God is enough!*

Only to sit and think of God,

Oh, what a joy it is!
To think the thought, to breathe the Name
Earth has no higher bliss.